10 Lifesaving Principles FOR WOMEN in Difficult Marriages

Karla Downing

Beacon Hill Press of Kansas City
Kansas City, Missouri

Copyright 2003
by Karla Downing

ISBN 083-412-050X

Printed in the
United States of America

Cover Design: Ted Ferguson

Library of Congress Cataloging-in-Publication Data

Downing, Karla, 1958-
    10 lifesaving principles for women in difficult marriages / Karla Downing.
        p. cm.
    ISBN 0-8341-2050-X (pbk.)
    1. Wives—Religious life. 2. Christian women—Religious life. 3. Marriage—Religious aspects—Christianity. I. Title: Ten lifesaving principles for women in difficult marriages. II. Title.

    BV4528.15.D69 2003
    248.8'435—dc21

                                                        2003009517

10   9   8   7   6   5   4   3   2

Contents

ACKNOWLEDGMENTS

To my husband, Monte, for being committed to our marriage through good times and bad, for giving me the time to pursue my dreams, and for letting me share our struggles to help others.

To my daughters: Kami and Rachel for being proud of me and for encouraging me. Lindsey for allowing me to be busy and still being excited about my book.

To my dad for bringing recovery into my life and for believing I could do anything I wanted.

To my mom for teaching me unconditional love and strong faith in the Lord.

To my mom and mother-in-law for taking care of all the things I didn't have time for.

To the Lord for salvation, grace, restoration of what the cankerworm and locust had eaten, and fulfilling His promise of a future and a hope.

To Debbie Falangas for sharing my passion for Christian women in difficult marriages and critiquing my ideas.

To all the women who have shared their pain and struggles with me; without them this book would not have been written.

To the rest of my family and friends: Gary, DeAnn, Mitch, Anita, Kristin, Gwen, Lori, and Miles for their encouragement through my struggles. Thanks for being there.

To Bob Noonan and Mike McMillan for allowing me to serve in the Steppin' Out recovery ministry. I have grown so much in the process.

To Scott Orth for reviewing my interpretation of scriptures on submission and divorce.

To my sponsors, Cindy and Gloria, for helping me apply these principles to my life.

To CLASServices for stirring my passion to write and showing me how to do it.

To my editors: Judith Perry and Kathy Ide for making an imperfect manuscript perfect.

To Beacon Hill Press of Kansas City: Thank you for sharing my vision to help women in difficult marriages.

Introduction

"I know the plans I have for you," declares the LORD,
"plans to prosper you and not to harm you,
plans to give you hope and a future."
—Jer. 29:11

*I*f you're a Christian woman in a difficult marriage, you're in a frustrating and confusing place. You've probably been told to love your husband, submit, pray, and wait. You've been there and done that. Nothing has changed. Where is God? Why doesn't He answer your prayers? Your heart breaks for your children as you see the effect your dysfunctional marriage is having on them.

Regardless of the specifics of the problems in your marriage, the toll it's taking on you is predictable. No doubt you often feel unloved and insecure. You may feel trapped, hopeless, alone, and even ashamed. You have trouble taking care of yourself and your children, because you're focused on your husband and the miseries of your relationship. It's sapping all of your energy to keep everything around you under control either by trying to force change or by being completely passive in order to keep an elusive peace that stays just out of your reach. Nothing in your life feels simple or spontaneous. The rest of the world seems to be paired off into happy couples. What happened to *your* happily-ever-after?

Sally doesn't believe in divorce, yet she's overcome with despair and hopelessness. Tearfully she confessed, "I feel so guilty. He was asleep on the couch, and it looked as if he weren't breathing. For a moment I hoped he wasn't. For just a moment I wished he were dead. And it was a relief. What's the matter with me?"

Some women cover for their husbands, pretending

everything's fine. Some women try to change their husbands to no avail. Some women believe there's no one else who is going through what they're going through. They don't know what to do. They can't live like this anymore, but they don't want a divorce.

The heart of this book comes from my own experience of being in a difficult marriage. I tried everything to force my husband to see the problem. I was angry, critical, and focused on him, unable to control my own behavior because I reacted to everything he did. Both of us were causing our children pain. The fruit of the Spirit was dying on the vine in my home.

In my journey I have learned to apply the principles I cover in this book. My marriage is healthier today, and I'm grateful that God restored it. I'm also grateful that He first brought me to a place of healing and understanding and that He wants me to be a woman of dignity—even in a difficult marriage.

My prayer is that the tools I share in this book will help you change your life. I won't try to tell you what to do. Marital relationships are complicated, and each marriage has its own dynamics. But I'll give you information, insights, principles, and ideas. Apply them to your situation as they work for you. If some of them don't apply or don't work for you, discard them. Don't discount the possibility of the need for professional counseling along the way.

Some of the principles will seem too difficult to do right away. That's OK. You'll grow into them. Taking it one day at a time, you can begin to change and heal. Your marriage may never be perfect. Few are. But your life and your marriage can change for the better—and you can have peace.

Lifesaving Principle

Understand Scriptural Truths

1

*Do your best to present yourself to God as one approved,
a workman who does not need to be ashamed
and who correctly handles the word of truth.*
—2 Tim. 2:15

*I*f you're navigating a difficult marriage, as a Christian you may struggle with how God feels about you. Do you sometimes wonder if He even cares about your struggles? Do you wonder if He's punishing you for marrying the wrong man? Is it too late to redeem your life? Does God even have a plan for you?

It's important for you to understand that in your quest to please God, even in the midst of a difficult marriage, it's not necessary to labor under common misconceptions about submission, marital rights, and your responsibilities.

God's Heart Toward You

The Israelites understood God's compassion toward them. They repeatedly turned their backs on Him by worshiping other gods. After long periods of suffering because God withheld blessings to them, they turned back to Him and prayed for forgiveness by reminding Him of His mercy: "You are a forgiving God, gracious and compassionate, slow to anger and abounding in love" (Neh. 9:17).

God forgives you for the mistakes you make. He cares about your problems and your pain. He's not punishing you, although you may be reaping the natural consequences of your choices. The love that led God to send Jesus to die on the Cross is the same love He has for you now. David tells us in Ps. 34:18, "The LORD is close to the brokenhearted and saves those who are crushed in spirit."

Even in your disappointment and sorrow, you can continue to trust in God's unfailing love and sovereign purpose, even if you don't understand why things have turned out the way they have. When you're broken and hurting, God's heart is soft and loving toward you.

Submission to Your Husband

Connie wants more than anything to obey God by submitting to her husband, Jeff. But Jeff wants to control everything—the money, the children, where she goes, who her friends are. He monitors what she watches on television and what she reads. He drops her off in front of the grocery store and waits in the car while she does the weekly shopping. Connie tells herself she's obeying God by quietly submitting to Jeff and his demands. She believes it would be out of God's will to demand that Jeff give her some space and the freedom to make decisions for herself.

Order in the Body

It's true that God has established order within the Body: Christ is the head of the Church, and the husband is the head of his wife and family. The husband is the head of the family in a structural way. Someone has to be in charge when there are impasses; however, that doesn't imply that the wife is not to be considered at all or that she's not allowed to participate in decisions. It was never intended that the husband would rule like a maniacal boss or a dictator. In the cooperative partnership of marriage, both individuals are highly valued and will have input into important decisions. The wife submits to her husband by respecting him, loving him, and trusting his decisions as long as they don't violate her conscience or God's Word.

Submission

A healthy husband-wife relationship is based on love and mutual respect, not obedience. Obedience implies a parent-child relationship. A woman brings to the marriage all her insight, talents, and viewpoints in order to complete her husband—including her ability to say no. The passage on submission, Eph. 5:22-24, has been misinterpreted to mean that a wife should submit to her husband in everything and that not submitting is *always* the same as disobeying God. But submission is always voluntary and can be withheld.

The Husband's Responsibilities

The husband, as the head of the home, has additional responsibilities. Eph. 5:25-26, 28-29, immediately following the submission verses, goes on to say, "Husbands, love your wives, just as Christ loved the church and gave himself up for her to make her holy. . . . In this same way, husbands ought to love their wives as their own bodies. He who loves his wife loves himself. After all, no one ever hated his own body, but he feeds and cares for it, just as Christ does the church."

Marriage is to be an example of Christ's relationship to the Church. The Church submits to Christ because He takes care of the Church and loves her. Therefore, submission by the wife goes hand in hand with her husband's responsibilities.

The assumption is that the husband will care for his wife in a loving way with her best interests in mind. One could also draw the assumption that the husband takes loving care of himself and his own body. In difficult marriages, these assumptions are likely false. Some husbands aren't capable of even loving themselves, which is demonstrated by destructive lifestyles. Can men who are alcoholics, workaholics, drug addicts, or women chasers be trusted to lead their families?

A man who loves his wife as Christ loved the Church will find his wife has no difficulty respecting him and placing herself under his authority. He can be trusted.

However, placing yourself under the authority of someone who does not love you or care for you can be dangerous. Col. 3:19 says, "Husbands, love your wives and do not be harsh with them." 1 Pet. 3:7 says, "Husbands, in the same way be considerate as you live with your wives, and treat them with respect as the weaker partner and as heirs with you of the gracious gift of life, so that nothing will hinder your prayers." This tells the husband to consider his wife's needs, to adapt to her, and to treat her with respect. Women respond naturally to husbands who treat them this way. But women have great difficulty being vulnerable with men who do not act lovingly toward them.

Paul's admonitions to the Church focused on what was culturally relevant at the time. Women were expected to submit to their husbands with respect. Men treated their wives as property; hence the emphasis on loving them, which was a radical concept in those days. Nowhere in these verses on love and submission does it say that men will never be required to submit and that women will never need to love.

Both husbands and wives are to cooperate and yield their rights and personal desires in order to preserve unity in the body and in their marriages.

Slaves and Slave Owners

In 1 Pet. 2:18, slaves are told to obey their masters: "Slaves, submit yourselves to your masters with all respect, not only to those who are good and considerate, but also to those who are harsh." Some have surmised that this example of submission to an unjust man implies that a wife should submit to her husband even if he is extremely harsh. There are several faults in that comparison. Peter is talking about a different relationship between slave and slave owner; the husband's responsibilities to his wife are much more comprehensive than those of the slave owner to the slave. We recognize that slavery is no longer morally acceptable—even though it was during Paul's time. We don't even condone the mistreatment of employees by their employers. In fact, in Eph. 6:5-9, Paul admonishes both the slaves and their masters to realize that they are "slaves of Christ, doing the will of God from your heart. Serve wholeheartedly, as if you were serving the Lord, not men" (vv. 6-7). These verses clearly highlight a reciprocal responsibility to do what's right and treat each other with respect.

Exceptions to Submission

We're also told to submit to authorities in government (Rom. 13:1-7), but with exceptions. When the government's order goes against God's commands, we do not obey. Peter was told by the authorities not to preach Christ, and he refused to obey, stating, "We must obey God rather than men!" (Acts 5:29). The apostle Paul was thrown into jail several times for disobeying the law by preaching. Hebrew midwives refused the Pharoah's command to kill the baby boys, because they feared God. God blessed them for it (Exod. 1:15-21). Following righteousness always comes before submission.

What if your husband asks you to put your family at risk or cause your children harm? Of course, you wouldn't do that. But what if he asks you to participate in activities that violate your conscience? Col. 3:18 says, "Wives, submit to your husbands, *as is fitting in the Lord*" (emphasis added).

Scripture clearly establishes that when a ruler or leader asks you to do something that goes against God's command, you're to disobey. When a husband's request is wrong, you can say no. This seems clear when we consider the "big things." If your husband asks you to murder his friend, you'll easily refuse. It gets more difficult when he asks you to sign for a loan you know you can't afford to repay. Here are some practical examples of times when it's acceptable for you to withhold submission:

- You know you need counseling to help your marriage, so you go to a counselor, even when your husband says not to.
- You refuse to watch pornographic movies.
- You do not give in to his demand to give up all activities, interests, and friends outside the marriage.
- You refuse to ride with him or to allow your children to ride in the car with him when he is driving while intoxicated.
- You refuse to allow illegal drugs in the house.

These are just a few examples. If you are being asked to submit in ways that you feel are wrong or that make you feel uncomfortable, pray, asking God for His wisdom.

Old Testament Examples

The Old Testament contains examples of women who did not obey their husbands. In the Book of Esther, Queen Vashti refused King Xerxes' request for her to come to his drunken feast to be looked at and admired by men. She no doubt knew he was drunk and didn't want to put herself in that position. She was willing to stand up for what was right at a great risk. In his anger and revenge, King Xerxes issued a royal decree deposing her as queen. Queen Esther dared several times to enter the king's presence without being summoned, which could have resulted in her being put to death if he had not extended his gold scepter to signal his approval. She risked her life by speaking against his top official, Haman, and the king's edict to kill the Jews. She was willing to disobey the king, her husband, for the higher good of saving her people from death. Abigail chose to disobey her husband to save lives by bringing David and his men the provisions Nabal had refused them (1 Sam. 25). God showed his approval of Abigail's actions by answering her prayer to punish Nabal.

When it's a matter of standing for what's good, standing against what's wrong, and protecting others and ourselves from harm, women need not submit to their husbands.

Abraham's wife, Sarah, leaves us with a conflicting example. "They were submissive to their own husbands, like Sarah, who obeyed Abraham and called him her master. You are her daughters if you do what is right and do not give way to fear" (1 Pet. 3:5-6). Sarah submitted to Abraham by moving from her home when God told Abraham to move from Haran to Canaan (Gen. 12:1-5). She agreed to lie twice when Abraham asked her to tell the Egyptian Pharaoh (Gen. 12:10-20) and King Abimelech (Gen. 20) that she was his sister. Abraham was afraid they would kill him in order to marry Sarah, since she was so beautiful. God inflicted diseases on Pharaoh's household and intervened by a dream with King Abimelech to prevent either of them from taking Sarah as his wife.

We're told to submit to our husbands as Sarah did but not to allow fear to rule us. Sarah let fear control her when she lied for Abraham. Abraham's motive for lying was his own fear and lack of trust in God. These lies would have brought about serious consequences if God had not miraculously intervened.

Sarah's submissive heart got out of hand. God intervened in Abraham's and Sarah's life, but He didn't have to. Sometimes He allows us to live with the consequences of our decisions.

Forfeiting of Headship

There's a difference between your husband's positional authority and his structural authority. Laurie Hall, in *An Affair of the Mind* (Wheaton, Ill.: Tyndale House Publishers, 1996), says, "The husband has positional authority. He occupies the office of the head of the home. If, in that office, he is serving his family members by truly loving and caring for them, he will also have functional authority. His family will naturally look to him to lead" (127). A man who behaves in a way that undermines his family, as in the case of addictions and abuse, forfeits his "functional authority to exercise his headship" (Ibid.).

What about men who use submission to demand their wives go along with them? Men can use the concept of submission to control, dominate, and manipulate their wives by saying things like "I'm the king of the castle. I will be treated special." This communicates an inner attitude that's self-serving rather than self-sacrificing. Paul Hegstrom in *Angry Men and the Women Who Love Them* (Kansas City: Beacon Hill Press of Kansas City, 1999), writes, "A man who treats 'his woman' like a servant, makes all the big decisions, and acts like master of the castle is exerting a type of abuse known as male privilege" (41).

The Bible clearly requires a high standard for the man, directing him to love his wife as Christ loves the Church. Christ was a servant. He did not come to be served, even though He was the King of glory. Our husbands are not to act like tyrants, commanding servants to give in to their every desire.

Hegstrom also writes, "Words like 'submission' and 'obey,' as well as other spiritual language and scripture, when taken out of context, typify a man who is actually spiritually abusing his wife. He probably has high regard for the patriarchal system and may say things like 'God gives me the right to do this. I'm the head of the family. I have all the rights in the world, and you have none'" (Ibid., 40). One of the common characteristics of an abuser is "He is a traditionalist believing in male supremacy and the stereotypical masculine sex role in the family. He feels he has the *right* to 'teach her a lesson'" (Ibid., 43). One of the common characteristics of an abused woman is that "she is a traditionalist about the home; strongly believes in family unity and the prescribed feminine sex role stereotype"

(Ibid., 44). This does not mean that every man and woman who believes in traditional roles in the family will misconstrue them—only that the beliefs can be taken advantage of when they're misapplied.

Use Judgment

Submission is not a rigid edict that prevents you from exercising control over any area of your life. Jesus cautioned us to be "as shrewd as snakes and as innocent as doves" (Matt. 10:16). Much damage has been done to women by taking a simplistic view of submission. If you're trying to please God in your marriage, look at whether or not you're obeying Him in all things. If you think the full extent of your responsibility in your marriage is to submit to your husband, then you may be ignoring other areas that are just as important and may even supersede submission, including your responsibility to stand up for righteousness and against evil.

Where's the Fruit?

Christians are supposed to bear good fruit—the fruit of the Spirit as described in Gal. 5:22-25 and also the fruit of our godly lives. Paul told the Ephesians to "live as children of light (for the light consists in all goodness, righteousness and truth)" (Eph. 5:8-9).

Are you producing fruit in your marriage? Are you producing the fruit of righteousness in your husband, your children, and yourself? Or is the result sin, envy, dissension, anger, and other evils? Does your husband continue in destructive behavior without consequences? Are you left feeling discouraged, angry, resentful, hurt, bitter, impatient, and discontented? Do you feel like a woman with dignity, or do you feel ashamed, beaten down, and broken? Are you taking action to expose sin and bring it to the light, or are you covering it up in the hope of keeping the peace for the time being?

In Gal. 5:19-21 Paul lists the acts of the sinful nature: "sexual immorality, impurity and debauchery; idolatry and witchcraft; hatred, discord, jealousy, fits of rage, selfish ambition, dissensions, factions and envy; drunkenness, orgies, and the like. I warn you, as I did before, that those who live like this will not inherit the kingdom of God." Then he goes on to list the fruit of the Spirit: "love, joy, peace, patience, kindness, goodness, faithfulness, gentleness and self-control" (Gal. 5:22-23).

Do you see your home in either of these lists? Passive tolerance of wrong in your difficult marriage will result in sin. It will produce anger, self-pity, careless words, worry, and unbelief. It can destroy physical health, dignity, and self-esteem. Children are provoked to anger and witness the poor handling of relationships—the only model of relationships they may ever see. Children in homes where the parents fight or have addictions are continually provoked to anger, and they carry that anger into their own marriages. If you're covering up for your husband in the interest of keeping the peace, you may actually be contributing to his self-destruction, because he never has to face the consequences of his actions.

Eph. 5:11 says, "Have nothing to do with the fruitless deeds of darkness, but rather expose them." Don't cover up and make excuses for evil. Gal. 6:7-9 says, "Do not be deceived: God cannot be mocked. A man reaps what he sows. The one who sows to please his sinful nature, from that nature will reap destruction; the one who sows to please the Spirit, from the Spirit will reap eternal life. Let us not become weary in doing good, for at the proper time we will reap a harvest if we do not give up." When you step in and intervene in God's law of reaping and sowing by not allowing your husband to face the consequences of his behaviors, you're acting out of fear and insecurity instead of trust and faith.

Jane and Bob have a secret: Bob is addicted to pornography. He spends hours on the computer every night, and Jane knows what he's doing. But she doesn't say a word. She worries that the kids will find the pornography on the computer, but she doesn't confront Bob and take a stand against his addiction. Jane is just biding her time, believing that her perseverance will be rewarded—someday.

Loving your husband may mean setting strong boundaries that say no to sin in his life, in your life, in your marriage, your home, and in your children's lives. God doesn't just leave us alone in our sin. He goes after us. He convicts us. If we persist, He allows us to suffer consequences and pain, and He disciplines us with the purpose of bringing us to repentance. Are you willing to hold your husband accountable? True, you aren't responsible for his choices, and he will have to give an account to God for his life. But *you* will give an account for *yours.*

Remember that 1 Pet. 3:17 tells us that if it is God's will for us to suffer, it's better to suffer for doing good than for doing evil. Doing the right thing is often not the easiest thing to do, but it's better to suffer for doing the right thing, knowing that you've pleased God.

Respect

Respect is necessary in a good relationship, and it's evidenced by showing honor and esteem toward the people you value. God instructed children to respect their parents (Lev. 19:3), the Israelites to respect the elderly (Lev. 19:32), slaves to respect their masters (Eph. 6:5), wives to respect their husbands (Eph. 5:33), the Church to respect elders and pastors (1 Thess. 5:12), and husbands to respect their wives (1Pet. 3:7).

In *Love Must Be Tough* (Waco, Tex.: Word, 1983), James Dobson explains that respect is a necessary part of love. It's human nature to value people who demand respect and devalue people who can be mistreated. He writes, "If there is hope for the dying marriages . . . then it is likely to be found in the reconstruction of *respect* between warring husbands and wives." You communicate how you expect to be treated by the boundaries you set. If you accept poor treatment and there is nothing that is completely "out of bounds," you may not get the respect you desire.

Unfortunately, there are men who believe that women are property that must be controlled. If your husband is such a man, it may be nearly impossible to gain his respect. However, even if your husband is a man who does not respect women, he may *value* you more if you set boundaries and demand that he abide by them.

Rights

You've been taught that as a Christian you must put your sinful nature to death, thereby dying to self and to sin. You die to self when you forgive, when you respond with gentleness to anger, when you choose right over wrong, when you stand for right even though you're afraid. You die to self when you serve others. But dying to self does not mean allowing someone to mistreat you without standing up for what's right.

If you allow your husband to mistreat you, how does that testify to your faith? If you endure mistreatment, are you promoting the gospel to your friends and family? If your husband is also a Christian, isn't his mistreatment of you hypocritical in your children's eyes? Taking a stand against sin even when there are negative consequences such as disapproval, risking the loss of your marriage, financial loss, or your husband's anger can be seen as a testimony to your faith.

Governments guarantee rights to their citizens. Paul reminded the Roman authorities twice that his rights as a Roman citizen were being violated (Acts 16:37; 22:25). The

United States was founded on the belief that her citizens have inalienable rights given by God—to life, liberty, and the pursuit of happiness. We consider ourselves entitled to the right to be considered innocent until proven guilty, to own property, to free speech, to freely assemble and worship. It is not inconsistent with Scripture to take a stand for what's just and right. Neither is it wrong for you to take a stand for your rights in your marriage.

Turn the Other Cheek

In Matt. 5:38-39 Jesus said, "You have heard that it was said, 'Eye for eye, and tooth for tooth.' But I tell you, do not resist an evil person. If someone strikes you on the right cheek, turn to him the other also." This scripture does not condone physical abuse or the tolerance of mistreatment. Jesus used this example to explain the differences between the Old Covenant and the New Covenant. Old Covenant law required an eye for an eye as punishment. Jesus explained that God cares about the heart more than superficial actions. He wants us to have an attitude of grace and forgiveness rather than an attitude of revenge.

Jesus went on to tell the disciples that they were to love not only their neighbors but their enemies (those who mistreated them) as well. 1 Pet. 3:9 says, "Do not repay evil with evil or insult with insult, but with blessing." Even if your husband treats you like an enemy, you can love him and treat him with courtesy and kindness while at the same time setting firm boundaries. Try to let go of any desire for revenge you might be harboring while still confronting the sin of evil attitudes and actions.

Christian Character Traits

"Sometimes I got tripped up by my own Christianity," Jessica told me. "I remember listening to sermons about being long-suffering and persevering through trials. But it seemed to me that the more 'Christian' I was—trying to love my husband, being gentle, submitting, persevering— the more emotionally and verbally abusive he became. When I finally started answering him back, I started getting his respect. I'm learning how to stand up for myself the right way."

What do long-suffering, forgiveness, gentleness, meekness, peace, and perseverance really mean in a difficult marriage?

Long-suffering

Long-suffering means not running out at the first hint of trouble. It means hanging in there even when you encounter problems in marriage. It doesn't mean giving up and accepting anything that comes your way—it means continuing to fight for what you know is right.

Perseverance

If you're going to contend for your marriage, do it in the right way, and refuse to passively accept anything and everything that happens. Always desire righteousness in your life.

Peace

It's tempting to keep the peace in your home by going along with your husband and walking on eggshells to keep from upsetting him. Rom. 12:18 tells us, "If it is possible, as far as it depends on you, live at peace with everyone." We're to do everything we can to have good relationships with the people in our lives. Doormats and physically and emotionally abused women do not have good relationships.

A Gentle and Quiet Spirit

Jesus described himself in Matt. 11:29 as gentle and humble in heart. Even in the midst of a difficult marriage, you can exhibit gentleness in your spirit, realizing that God is in control, rather than manifesting turmoil and rebellion.

Quietness refers to an inner peace and strength where you can confidently rest, trusting God. Being quiet in your spirit doesn't preclude you from speaking the truth or confronting and resisting evil.

Forgiveness

Don't confuse forgiveness with passive tolerance, thinking it means acceptance of everything without boundaries. Forgiveness has nothing to do with willingly tolerating mistreatment or withholding consequences. It means we give up our right to take revenge.

A New Foundation

If unquestioned submission always resulted in godliness, I would say, "By all means, submit." But passive acceptance of mistreatment and sin leads to brokenness, pain, disrespect, difficulties for your children, physical health problems, wasted lives, and emotional damage. And in the long run, it often results in divorce anyway. Understanding and applying the lifesaving principles described in this book can help you take a stand for righteousness by obeying God and submitting to Him above all else.

Lifesaving Principle

Reach Out

Two are better than one, because they have a good return
for their work: If one falls down, his friend can help him up.
But pity the man who falls and has no one to help him up!
—Eccles. 4:9-10

Women who are suffering in difficult marriages often find themselves withdrawing from their normal routines and activities, from friends, and sometimes even from their families. Do you see yourself in any of the following reasons women isolate themselves?

- You're embarrassed, and you don't want anyone to know the truth about your marriage.
- Your life is so overwhelming that you don't have energy for outside interests.
- You think no one would understand what you're going through or why you put up with it.
- You've confided in someone before and have been hurt or disappointed by the response you've received.
- You're afraid to leave home for very long at a time, because there's no telling what your spouse might do if you're not there to take care of things.
- Your husband doesn't want you to have friends or activities outside the home.
- Your husband tells you to keep your marriage problems private.

As tempting as it is to remain isolated and try to keep your problems to yourself, the truth is that isolation keeps you stuck in the same spot. It's imperative that you have a support system and a life outside your marriage.

Breaking Out of Isolation

The first steps out of isolation may take you outside your comfort zone and may even be scary, but it's important for you to realize that you're not alone. There are many women whose marriages are not as difficult as yours, and there are many women whose marriages are much worse than yours. The reason you feel your situation is unique and that you're alone is because these women are keeping quiet about their problems too. It's essential that you find people who understand what's happening in your life so that they can support you. Yes, it will take courage to admit that you've been pretending and that your life is really not OK. But you must do it anyway. Admitting your faults, problems, and weaknesses to others is an important part of healing (James 5:13-16).

Support from Family and Friends

Family members and close friends may not always be the best people to offer you support, and it will be very difficult for them to remain neutral. Often their comments will be "Don't put up with it! Leave him! I would never put up with that. You deserve better!" Reactions along these lines will end up leaving you feeling embarrassed because you *are* putting up with it. Just remember: even though they mean well, it's a lot easier to tell someone to leave a marriage than it is to actually do so. Many persons eventually end up tolerating a situation they swore they *wouldn't* tolerate.

So choose carefully how many details you tell about your marriage. Let your comfort level and your family's ability to handle it be your guide. Knowing a lot of detail about your husband could result in your family being unable to be civil to him, which could cause even more problems in your marriage.

Whether or not to tell his family and friends about his problems is another decision you'll have to make. Family allegiance is very strong, and his family may be unable to accept the truth and will blame you instead. If this happens, it can add to your isolation. Your husband's reaction to you telling his family may also add more stress to your marriage.

Church Support

Early in my marriage when I was in a lot of pain, I told my women's Bible study group about my marriage problems. The study group's pat advice was "Let Jesus be your Husband." I felt guilty for failing to be satisfied with just Jesus and questioned whether I was even wrong to feel pain in my marriage.

The teachings given in Christian seminars and Bible studies usually apply to healthy marriages and are hard to apply to a difficult, troubled marriage. I remember feeling frustrated and disillusioned, and I vowed never to read another book or attend another seminar on marriage. Tracy expressed her frustration with well-intentioned ministry leaders by saying, "If one more Christian tells me to just love my husband, I'm going to scream. I'll never again tell my problems to someone who hasn't experienced what I'm experiencing."

Suggestions like "Pray for God to change him" and "Love your husband" are often misunderstood by women in difficult marriages to mean "Tolerate mistreatment and don't hold him accountable for his behavior." Prov. 25:20 says, "Like one who takes away a garment on a cold day, or like vinegar poured on soda, is one who sings songs to a heavy heart." If you're getting advice from well-meaning people who don't understand the complexities of difficult marriages and it's causing you to be even more miserable, you're getting advice from the wrong people.

The following things may prevent you from admitting the truth about your marriage. Do you feel your husband's sin is a reflection on you? Are you responding to him in ways that are embarrassing to admit? Perhaps everyone thinks he's a wonderful man or you think others have wonderful marriages, so you feel alone. Unable to tell the truth, you keep your pain and shame to yourself and put up a front and pretend everything is fine.

Pastors, church leaders, and church members vary in their ability to give support to women in difficult marriages. Some pastors realize the benefits of support groups and refer their members to them, and others are starting support groups at their own churches. Some of these pastors are knowledgeable about abuse, addictions, dysfunction, and so on; others are not.

Always be willing to reach out to your church for support, but remember that staff there may not have the same training as professional counselors, and you may need additional help to deal with your marriage.

Professional Help

Counseling can give you helpful, professional insight into your problems. "Plans fail for lack of counsel, but with many advisers they succeed" (Prov. 15:22). "He who walks with the wise grows wise" (Prov. 13:20). There is a time for getting wisdom from those who have special training.

Try to find a counselor who is experienced in dealing with your particular problem. If you're dealing with abuse in your marriage, find a counselor who has insight into abusive relationships. If addiction is destroying your marital relationship, find a counselor who has a deep understanding of addiction. If your husband agrees to go to counseling with you, the counselor should still see each of you alone occasionally so that you can each be honest about your difficulties without fear of retribution from your spouse. If your husband refuses to go for counseling, don't hesitate to go alone.

Counselors use different approaches, so it's important you find a counselor who employs a style that works for you. Some focus on your past as a key to your present. Others focus on dealing with your situation today and finding practical solutions. Some counselors do more listening than others.

While going to a Christian counselor is good in theory, it's not always practical. Some insurance companies do not cover the use of Christian counselors, and many people can't afford to pay cash for therapy. Non-Christian counselors have been trained to help with interpersonal relationships and have knowledge and insights that can help you. Going to a non-Christian counselor is better than not going at all. You'll need to reconcile what any counselor tells you with your faith. Use discernment, and discard what's not scriptural.

If you've had counseling that was not successful in the past, don't give up. Maybe you were with the wrong counselor. Maybe you weren't really ready to hear what the counselor told you. But regardless of your past experience, don't give up on counseling as an option for getting help.

Finding a good counselor may take some work. Ask your physician or people you know for referrals. Check with your church to see if a referral network is available. An important step is to find out if counseling is a covered benefit on your medical insurance or through your employer. If you don't have insurance coverage, ask the counselor if he or see will charge on a sliding scale so you can afford to pay. And never hesitate to change counselors if the one you are seeing isn't helping you.

Support Groups

If you've isolated yourself because you feel that no one else can understand your problems, it's hard to see your way out of your situation. Attending a support group can be a significant step in learning to value yourself and building a better life. One of the first things you'll say to yourself is "I'm *not* crazy! There are other women who have the same feelings and problems I have."

You'll gain hope from other women who have been where you are and have improved their lives. You'll learn new ways to handle the day-to-day struggles you face. Even when you share with them incidents and feelings that show your worst side, you'll feel accepted. You'll have someone to call when you need support between meetings. No one will tell you what to do—they're simply there to share your experience and struggle. Those who have been where you are can be empathetic and helpful. It's not an instant cure but rather the beginning of a life-changing process.

Many support groups are available. They include 12-step groups like Al-Anon, Codependents Anonymous, Codependents of Sex Addicts, Gam-Anon, and Nar-Anon Family Groups. There are also Christian-based 12-step programs such as Overcomers Outreach. The thread that ties these programs together is the 12 steps and the support you'll receive. All 12-step programs are based on anonymity and confidentiality. What you talk about in meetings is not disclosed to outsiders. If you don't know of such a program in your area, try calling larger churches and asking if the staff is aware of local support groups, or you can go to the phone book or the Internet.

The 12 steps are based on scriptural principles and a belief in God. Some Christians are not comfortable with the group's reference to God as simply "a Higher Power." As a result, some churches have started their own programs that acknowledge God as Father, Son, and Holy Spirit.

Not all churches and pastors support recovery programs. Some say you need only one step: salvation. But the truth is that most people need more support. Getting saved does not instantly remove all of life's problems. Just as it's not wrong to go to a medical doctor for physical problems, it's not wrong to go to support groups for help with emotional, spiritual, and marital problems.

Go to several meetings, if necessary, until you find one that's the size and personality mix that allows you to feel comfortable. Then make a commitment to attend a weekly meeting. Make the meeting a part of your normal schedule. Once your family gets used to your being gone on a particular day or evening, you'll not be inclined to make excuses for not attending.

A note of warning: Don't stop attending your support group when your husband makes small changes. Husbands will sometimes make slight, temporary changes in the hope that their wives will give up. The wife will accept the small change, feeling relieved that the problem is on its way to being history. The truth is, difficult marital problems, like the ones you have, don't disappear quickly or easily. Stick with your support group.

When Your Husband Says "No"

Your husband may attempt to talk you out of your support group, thereby keeping you isolated. He may tell you that's it's disloyal to talk about your problems. As long as your motive is pure—meaning it's not to discredit or destroy him out of anger or revenge—and you're doing it for the good of your marriage and family or to take care of yourself, it's not betrayal. Staying quiet to cover for him is not a good reason to keep silent. In fact, it's often the secrecy that surrounds a difficult marriage that allows the unhealthy cycle to continue. The secrecy protects your spouse from facing the truth, suffering the consequences, and being accountable. Let your husband know that you're not attending your support group to talk about him but to get help for yourself so that you can be a better person, wife, and mother.

The Differences Between Healthy and Unhealthy Relationships

Even the best marriages are not perfect and endure a certain amount of adjustment and conflict. Working out differences requires good communication, cooperation, and compromise.

Healthy marriages are composed of two individuals who are healthy, independent adults with the ability to love and receive love, respect and accept each other, resolve conflict, communicate directly and honestly, trust, and take responsibility for their own choices and actions. Both partners value the relationship and feel secure.

Difficult marriages are composed of two unhealthy individuals whose personal problems interfere with their ability to interact in the ways described above. There is competition, struggle for control, unresolved conflict, hostility and anger, disrespect, distrust, lack of acceptance, irresponsibility, and blame placing. The marriage is strained and unhappy.

In difficult marriages arguments frequently follow the same pattern regardless of the actual issue at hand. Paula tried to talk to her husband about his rude treatment of her the night before. He shifted the argument and began telling her that she was overly sensitive and critical. Paula tried to defend herself and ended up getting angry. The problem—his rudeness—was never really discussed and certainly not resolved. They both walked away feeling angry, unloved, and alienated.

Types of Difficult Marriages

You probably are well aware of what behavior is destroying your marriage. There are various addictions and behaviors, personality disorders, mental illnesses, physical illnesses, abuses, and other unhealthy relationship patterns that contribute. Learn all you can about what you're dealing with. There are books, support groups, the Internet, counselors, and other resources that can help in your research. If you're not sure what you're up against, talk to a counselor to put a label on the problem.

Addictions. An addict is one who is obsessed with altering his or her mind in order to cope. It could be with alcohol, drugs, gambling, sex, pornography, work, or anything used repeatedly to escape feelings and problems. King

Solomon advised the avoidance of anything to excess. "Listen, my son, and be wise, and keep your heart on the right path. Do not join those who drink too much wine or gorge themselves on meat, for drunkards and gluttons become poor, and drowsiness clothes them in rags" (Prov. 23:19-21).

Addicts are self-centered, unable to empathize, emotionally immature, unreliable, resentful, dishonest, unreasonable, and blaming. These characteristics are often present even when the addict is not using his or her drug of choice, called the "dry drunk syndrome."

Until addicts are ready to face their addictions, they will adamantly deny reality, blaming their problems on someone else—most frequently a spouse.

Drug and Alcohol Addictions. A drug addict or alcoholic is someone who can't stop drinking or using drugs. He or she does not have to drink or use drugs every day to be addicted. In fact, many drug addicts and alcoholics are periodic users, using only on weekends or periodically for days at a time. They can be successful in business and do fairly well at holding their lives together, at least for a while.

Sexual Addictions. Sexual addiction refers to an excessive and obsessive focus on sex. It can include looking at pornography, frequent masturbation, phone sex, participating in Internet sex chat rooms, prostitution, or involvement in many affairs. The sex addict usually withdraws, acts out, and then is filled with shame and fear over the behavior. The cycle then repeats itself. Sex is a very powerful stimulant that leaves lasting mental images on the brain. The sex addict becomes hooked on the chemical stimulation associated with the stimulus. Sex addicts tend to be emotionally withdrawn in relationships, have difficulty with intimacy, and are unable to deal with feelings and conflict.

Gambling. Gambling is classified as an addiction due to the loss of control and the addictive nature of the behavior.

The typical lying, denial, anger, blame, and unpredictability that result from an addiction accompany it. The gambler has difficulty stopping, even when all the money is gone. Many lose everything, including their families. As Solomon said, "He who works his land will have abundant food, but he who chases fantasies lacks judgment (Prov. 12:11).

Workaholism and Other Excesses. The workaholic uses work to avoid dealing with emotional and relationship issues that he or she finds uncomfortable. The workaholic has no time for family and is emotionally unavailable. His or her spouse takes on most of the household and child-rearing duties. Some become addicted to a particular sport or a multitude of outside interests that keep them occupied. Workaholism or other excesses may sound simple compared to other problems, but the lack of emotional connection is very painful for the spouse.

Abuse. Physical, emotional, and verbal abuse are all demeaning and destructive. Prov. 14:17 says, "A quick-tempered man does foolish things, and a crafty man is hated." If you're afraid of your husband, you may be in an abusive relationship. An abusive man usually feels threatened by his wife and refuses to cooperate with her, because he fears losing control or power over her. The abuse is designed to keep his wife in line or acting in a way that feels comfortable to him. He often uses punishment to teach her a lesson.

Anger. Anger is destructive when it is in excess or acted out in sinful ways. Prov. 15:18 says, "A hot-tempered man stirs up dissension, but a patient man calms a quarrel." It's difficult to feel safe and valued by an angry man.

Passive-aggressive anger, while subtle, is damaging. The passive-aggressive man does not admit he's angry. Fearing dependency on his wife, he doesn't view her as an equal partner. He mistakes conflict and criticism as an attack on him and readily defends himself. He's unable to look at himself introspectively and see that he could be wrong. He does things out of anger but denies he did them: being late, forgetting her requests, not showing up, doing something the wrong way, or doing what she asks him not to do—all purposefully. He holds resentments. He may tell his wife that she's in control of the relationship and responsible for everything, but in reality she has no control, because he thwarts and outmaneuvers her at every turn.

General Dysfunction. If your spouse is disagreeable or controlling and unable to discuss issues, resolve conflicts, cooperate with you, or listen to your concerns, you're in an unhealthy relationship pattern, and your marriage is difficult. Although these patterns vary in the degree of severity, the dysfunction will not go away until you and your partner learn to deal with them in a healthy way.

Physical Problems. Chronic or permanent physical illness causes stress and imbalance in a marriage. It can be difficult to draw lines regarding responsibilities and emotional reactions like anger and moodiness when an underlying physical problem is present. Adults with learning disabilities or attention deficit disorder may have difficulty following through, listening, being responsible, and controlling impulses and emotions. It may seem that the kind thing to do is to take over their responsibilities. If your husband uses an illness as an excuse to avoid responsibilities or to mistreat family members, it's important that you hold him accountable for getting help.

Sudden changes in personality and emotions can be related to physical illnesses. If you think this may be the case with your husband, it's important for you to confront him and encourage him to get a medical checkup.

Mental Illness. Mental illness can cause grave difficulties in a marriage. One of the most common mental illnesses is *bipolar disease,* also known as manic-depressive disease. A person suffering from this condition experiences periods of extreme depression or mania. You will notice extreme mood changes. Drugs or alcohol are often used to mask highs and lows to help the individual feel more normal.

Narcissism is a form of self-centeredness that's common in addicts, alcoholics, and abusive men. However, a severe form is diagnosed as narcissistic personality disorder and is characterized by an exaggerated self-image, a feeling of being special, expectations of special treatment, a need to be admired, a tendency to use people, an inability to be empathetic, and an arrogant attitude.

It's not your job to diagnose whether or not your husband suffers from a mental illness. A qualified psychologist or medical doctor will have to do that. The good news is that medication can control many mental illnesses.

Keep in mind that even though mental illness is not something your husband has a choice about, you must still protect yourself and your children and maintain a decent quality of life by demanding that your husband get the help he needs.

The Roller Coaster

Difficult marriages are often referred to as roller-coaster rides because things change so quickly, and the highs and lows are extreme. There are periods when the ride is smooth, but you know that another bumpy period is waiting just around the corner.

Tammy is married to an alcoholic who goes through periods of drinking heavily and mistreating everyone in the home. At other times, he's a good dad and husband, and they have fun together. He has a successful career and is good at several sports. Tammy loves his sense of humor and his ability to take over when she feels insecure, but she hates it when he drinks and gets in his moods—sometimes lasting for weeks at a time. Each time that their relationship returns to normal and all is well, she believes the worst is behind them. It always shocks her when the drinking starts again. Tammy doesn't know which side of her husband is real—the good guy or the bad guy.

The truth is, both sides of her husband are real. When Tammy accepts that and reconciles herself to the fact that the drinking and mood swings will reappear, she'll be less surprised when the bad times come, and she'll be able to deal with her husband more effectively.

It's the not knowing when things will blow up again that keeps you in a constant state of insecurity and nervousness. Are you spending most of your time and energy trying to figure things out? It's important to understand the problem as well as you can, but ultimately you have to take care of yourself.

Lifesaving Principle 3

Change Yourself, Not Him

Each one should test his own actions. Then he can take pride
in himself, without comparing himself to somebody else,
for each one should carry his own load.
—Gal. 6:4-5

*Y*ou will stand before the Lord one day and give an account of your life. But you will not be required to account for your husband's actions.

For years I tried to make my husband better, as if I would be giving an account of his life to God. I spent so much energy trying to make him into a good Christian husband that I fell short of being the Christian wife God intended me to be. 2 Cor. 5:10 says, "We must all appear before the judgment seat of Christ, that each one may receive what is due him for the things done while in the body, whether good or bad." Jesus said in Matt. 12:36, "I tell you that men will have to give account on the day of judgment for every careless word they have spoken." I spoke thousands of careless words in anger and desperation that I will have to answer for. One day I decided I did not want to add any more to that number.

When you give your account, God will want to know what you did as the steward of all He has given you—time, money, trials, opportunities, freedom, knowledge, the Bible, salvation, family, and relationships (Matt. 25:14-30). He's not going to ask you to explain your husband's choices, nor will He allow you to use your husband's choices as an excuse for your own.

How Do You Change Yourself?

Your life would improve if your husband would change. There's no doubt about that. And no doubt you expend an enormous amount of your energy trying to change him. You're focused on his problem: understanding it, fixing it, coping with it, covering up for it. You may try to manipulate his choices so that he does the right things: goes to work, controls the drinking or drug use, treats you and the children right, pays the bills. You've tried nagging, explaining, pleading, threatening. You've searched for just the right words to help him see the problem. You're completely focused on fixing him. What he's doing dominates your thinking, your emotions, and your choices.

Does this sound like you? If you're focusing on finding the key to changing him—either on your own or through God's miraculous intervention—you're neglecting the only thing you *can* change: your own life.

In order to bring about positive change in your own life, the focus must shift from your husband to yourself. It's common for women in difficult marriages to become so enmeshed in trying to control their husband's behavior that they get completely out of touch with what their own feelings are. You probably can tell at a glance what your husband's mood is. How long has it been since you focused on what you think or feel or feel like doing?

Jesus said in Matt. 7:3-5 that we need to deal with our own faults and sins before we point to faults in others. Because the human tendency is to be less tolerant of faults in others than in ourselves, He reminded us that we could be pointing to a "speck" in someone else's eye, all the while having a "plank" in our own. Calling us hypocrites, He warned us to "first take the plank out of your own eye, and then you will see clearly to remove the speck from your brother's eye." By making a conscious effort to take the focus off your husband and put it on you, you begin to pay attention to your own feelings, thoughts, choices, and needs, which are the only things you can change. Once you focus on changing yourself, you'll be able to clearly point to things your husband does with a pure conscience and a clearer understanding of the true problem, not to condemn him but to hold him responsible for his own actions. Remember—when the burden of responsibility is reversed, God sees him as having a plank in his eye and you as having a speck.

Let's talk about some ways you can effect change, starting with yourself.

Give Up Being a Victim or a Martyr

Do you feel like your husband's victim—hopeless and trapped? Well, you're really not his victim. You dated him and married him voluntarily. Maybe you're staying in your marriage because of the vows you took and you feel it's the right thing to do. But it's crucial that you recognize that you still have the choice to leave or to stay. Recognizing that you have choices helps you change your attitude toward your circumstances. Victims are resentful and helpless and blame others for their problems. You don't have to be a victim.

Have you fallen into the role of martyr? A martyr willingly suffers and sacrifices. A martyr says, "I don't need more out of life. I'm staying for the kids. I'm enduring and waiting like a good wife should." Martyrs expect to be pitied for their suffering and applauded for their sacrifices. They're willing to suffer because they're unwilling to take responsibility for their choices and initiate change. This is not to say that sacrifice is wrong, but martyrdom is unhealthy if done for the wrong motives. Prov. 21:29 says, "A wicked man puts up a bold front, but an upright man gives thought to his ways."

Letting go of being a victim and a martyr allows you to give thought to your ways, recognize that you have choices, and take full responsibility for those choices. Shedding these roles empowers you to move toward being an adult in control of your own life.

Let Go of the Obsession

If you're obsessed with your husband and his behavior, you're giving him control over your life. When you're obsessed, you focus on one thing to the exclusion of everything else, and this causes difficulty in other areas of your life. You may find it nearly impossible to concentrate on your job, the kids, and necessary daily tasks. One woman married to a sex addict explained it this way: "My mind is mush. I can't stop thinking about him and what he's doing. I can't even work. I just can't let him go, even though I want to."

When I find myself obsessed with things, I find that no matter how hard I try not to think about the problem, it continually grabs my attention. I'm like a prisoner—a prisoner of my own thoughts who's forced to endure emotional turmoil and expend energy without my permission. My thoughts repeatedly return to the obsession throughout the day and in the middle of the night, making it difficult to attend to other things in my life, even the things that matter most.

When my middle daughter was six years old, she told her grandmother that she wished someone would read her the Bible and answer her questions but that her mommy and daddy were too busy fighting. "They don't notice me," she said. This helped me see how obsessed I was with my husband. Even though training my children in the Lord was one of my deepest desires, my obsession with my husband robbed me of the ability to take care of the one thing that mattered most. Obsession is a jealous master, and it prevents us from managing our lives.

Letting go of obsession does not come easily. God wants us to control our thoughts and not be controlled or mastered by them (1 Cor. 6:12). You can help yourself stop thinking about your husband by refusing to allow yourself to do the things that get you hooked, like watching him, checking up on him, and asking questions. Stop doing anything that gives you information to be obsessed with. Holly couldn't concentrate on her work or her son's homework because she was thinking about Ken and why he was late from work. *Where is he? What is he doing? Why did he leave work early? Why did he ask me for money this morning?* She put her work down and started making phone calls to Ken's friends. She felt certain he was somewhere drinking again, but she had to know. The source of Holly's obsession was allowing herself to watch her husband and actively think about what he was doing. She was obsessed with finding out whether or not her husband was drinking by thinking about him, watching him, second-guessing his actions, and looking for evidence to substantiate her fears—and she was losing her peace of mind in the process.

Try to control your thoughts by forcing yourself to think about other things. God tells us we can choose what we think about (Phil. 4:8-9). With divine power at our disposal, we're capable of taking every thought captive "to make it obedient to Christ" (2 Cor. 10:5).

Admit That You're Powerless

Why do we become obsessed with our husbands? Because we believe that if we can force them to change, everything will be OK. I frantically tried to get my husband to see his problem. I put so much energy into it that I ignored my children, my career, my friends, and my relationship with God.

You want to believe there is something you can do to fix your husband, and you think it's your responsibility to fix him. His problem directly affects you in so many ways that it's understandable that you want him to change. If he didn't drink or take drugs or get angry or act up or gamble, you would naturally be happier. Your fears about the future are well-founded, and anxiety and worry are natural responses to the uncertainty you live with daily. But there's nothing you can do to force him to change, and all of your vain attempts are draining you of the energy you need to improve your own life. Your efforts to change him actually make the situation worse and keep you stuck.

You must admit that you're completely powerless to accomplish what you want. You're 100 percent powerless over other people's choices, behaviors, feelings, reactions, attitudes, decisions, thoughts, and addictions. Control is an illusion; in fact, it's as useless as standing on the beach and commanding the ocean waves to stop. God created each of us with free will. He does not force us to do anything, even when He knows it's in our best interest. If God doesn't force His creation to change by using His power to control us, why do you think you can force your husband to change?

When you try to force change in others by exerting control, you ultimately lose control over your own life. I was so busy trying to get my husband to change that I was tolerating things in my own behavior that were wrong—and I should have recognized that. Instead of taking control of my own life, I was merely *reacting* to him. Many times I told him that he was wrong, yet I was doing the same thing I was accusing him of.

Trying to control your husband can result in overt behavior: nagging, arguing, suggesting, getting angry. It can also be covert: keeping the peace by placating and pretending that everything is all right and arranging things to prevent upsetting him. All of these behaviors boil down to the same thing—manipulation. When you covertly or overtly control, you assume you know what's best for your husband. Only God knows what's in his heart and what it will take to soften and change him. Although God will not force him to change, He will work in his life in the way He knows is best. When you admit that you're powerless over your husband, you're stepping aside and letting God take over.

Fear is likely the silent motivator behind your compulsion to control. Many of your fears are no doubt valid and reasonable. Yet to react to those fears by trying to control your husband instead of trusting God is a losing proposition.

Understand Your Past

As adults, we tend to marry people with whom we replay the familiar patterns of our childhood, because we are most comfortable with those dynamics. For example, if your mother kept the peace at all costs and never confronted problems, you may do the same in your marriage. If you were afraid to speak up as a child or were ignored when you did, you may be afraid to speak up now. Women who were physically or sexually abused as children find men who are abusive. Those of us who grew up with denial in our homes tend to deny reality as adults.

You may be thinking, *My home wasn't dysfunctional. My parents loved me and had a good marriage.* However, you may come to see that there were patterns in your home that made you comfortable with your husband's problems and predisposed you to being attracted to him.

There's also a tendency to marry someone who's at the same level emotionally. Until you change the problems within yourself, you'll probably seek out the same type of man. It's common to feel an attraction for someone who seems familiar and comfortable. Emotionally healthy people usually attract emotionally healthy mates. Unhealthy people bring their unresolved issues and impaired relationship skills into their marriages.

No matter what your husband's problems are, you're partially responsible for the overall marriage difficulties. He may drink, abuse drugs, have anger control problems, behave abusively, but you probably react and thereby enable him. Even passively tolerating abuse or mistreatment makes you partially responsible, because you're allowing it to continue.

Weak boundaries or no boundaries in the marital relationship contribute to the problems. Some women are too dependent or too independent because of a fear of being vulnerable. Some have low self-esteem and are drawn to men who mistreat them because they don't feel worthy of being treated better. Some women don't know what they want or are afraid to make decisions, so they marry controlling men who handle everything for them.

Do you understand your past? Think about your childhood. Talk to your parents and siblings about your home. Did you protect your mother or father? Did you feel responsible for your parents or your siblings? Was there an addiction or dysfunction in your family? Were you sexually, verbally, or physically abused? Your goal is to come to a place of understanding about the type of family you grew up in, what your role in your family was, and how that affects who you are today.

Second, look at the male-female relationships in your past, and try to determine what type of men you've been attracted to. Is there a pattern? Were they passive or controlling? Did they have addictions? Did they treat you with respect? Did you feel insecure and unloved? Did you tend to be controlling or controlled? Did you take on too much responsibility or too little? Did you pick men who need to be "fixed"? Were you too dependent or too independent? Are you an independent, healthy adult with your own thoughts, goals, and interests, or are you dependent on others to make a life for you?

As you think about your childhood and past relationships, you may begin to see patterns that give you insight into why you chose your husband and why you react to the problems in your marriage the way you do.

Feel Your Emotions

Once you successfully take the obsession off your husband and focus more on yourself and your past, you'll become aware of many new feelings.

Emotions that you're feeling today are not necessarily related to what's happening today. Have you ever had a memory from your childhood that was triggered by a smell? Suddenly you experience the emotions you felt all those years ago. You have little control over the emotion or how intense it is. Anger can work that way too. Psychologists call it projection. You might feel extreme anger toward the person in front of you at the checkout line, but in reality you're angry with your husband.

Women in difficult marriages feel many intense emotions: fear, frustration, hopelessness, regret, guilt, disappointment, shame—just to name a few. Those emotions are uncomfortable, but they have to be felt and dealt with. God created you to feel. Feelings give you insight into your life by showing you what's in your heart and how things are affecting you.

Feelings are directly related to your thoughts. If your husband forgets to call you to tell you he's going to be late from work, you may feel angrier as time goes on. If you focus on the possibility that he's been in a car accident, you'll feel fear and anxiety. If you acknowledge that you don't know what he's doing, you might feel only mild concern or curiosity, thinking he probably has a good reason for being late. Your thoughts about the situation will affect your feelings. Solomon warns us not to be "quickly provoked in your spirit" (Eccles. 7:9). Becoming aware of your thoughts will help you control your reactions, which is what God holds us accountable for.

Feelings and emotions in and of themselves are not sinful. It's what you do with your emotions that can be sin. You can be angry without sinning (Eph. 4:26). Feeling anger toward someone is not sin, but lashing out at the person is. Jesus felt compassion, anger, sadness, grief, and joy, yet He controlled His responses to these feelings and remained without sin. David described many feelings in the Psalms: fear, depression, joy, disappointment, sadness, despair, and confusion. Yet he decided what to do with those feelings. In Ps. 42:5-6 he described himself as depressed, saying, "Why are you downcast, O my soul? Why so disturbed within me?" Then he chose his thoughts and response by saying, "Put your hope in God, for I will yet praise him, my Savior and my God." He acknowledged his despair and depression and then chose to trust God.

It's critical to your emotional, spiritual, and physical health that you pay attention to your feelings. Stuffing or denying feelings is unhealthy and is one reason many women in difficult marriages become physically ill with ulcers, colitis, depression, migraines, chronic fatigue, high blood pressure, nerve problems, and other symptoms doctors label as psychosomatic or stress related. In order to change your behavior, you must be aware of your underlying feeling in any situation. Recognize it, identify it, accept it, and decide what you want to do with it.

It's not easy to choose your responses. Learning to react with the fruit of the Spirit is difficult. In Rom. 7 Paul wrote that he found himself battling the temptation to do what he didn't want to do. Self-control is hard to maintain when you're living in a difficult marriage. You're continually dealing with many complex issues and emotions. Thankfully, Paul ends with Rom. 8:1, stating that there's no condemnation for us in Christ because we have been set free from the law of sin. 1 John 1:9-10 says, "If we confess our sins, he is faithful and just and will forgive us our sins and purify us from all unrighteousness. If we claim we have not sinned, we make him out to be a liar, and his word has no place in our lives." God is aware of your sin nature that's continually warring in your heart if you've not yet allowed His Holy Spirit to cleanse and sanctify your heart. He's always ready to forgive.

Own Your Feelings

Once you become aware of your feelings, you must be willing to own them and not blame your husband for how you feel. How many times have you heard someone say something like "You make me so angry" or "You make me crazy" or "You make me feel guilty" or "You make me sick"? Actually, no one *makes* anyone feel anything. How we feel at any moment is affected by who we are: our past, our expectations, our physical state, our personality, the meaning we attach to the experience, and our state of mind.

Normally, you easily tolerate your child's tantrums or whining, but occasionally you find yourself responding harshly. Those are probably the days when you're physically and/or emotionally tired and overwhelmed. Your state of mind affects how you respond at that moment. It's not the child's tantrum that makes you respond harshly but a weakened emotional or physical state of mind.

Some people are naturally patient and meek, while others are naturally assertive. This personality "filter" predisposes you to react a certain way to events and other people.

Past experiences affect how you respond. As a child, I was the only one in my family who got angry and pointed out the truth about problems in my family. I brought a mind-set into my marriage that contributed to my desire to control everything. My past and my personality contributed to my perception of events as threatening.

Owning your own emotions involves accepting responsibility for your feelings, perceptions, and reactions. Your specific reactions and perceptions are unique to you. If you picked 100 women at random, and they were all married to your husband, would each of them respond exactly the way you do to everything he says and does? Would the same things bother them to the same degree they bother you? Don't be tempted to think of the obvious bad things he does and say yes, because each of those 100 women would consider even the worst things either more offensive or less offensive than you do.

Communicate in "'I' statements" when telling your husband how you feel. Remember—your goal is to tell him the effect his behavior has on you and how it makes you feel, not to control him, force him to change, or make him see things your way. "'You' statements" blame him for how you interpreted his action, placing the responsibility on him for your feelings. Here are some examples of "'I' statements" versus "'you' statements":

- "You were rude to me" vs. "I felt hurt by your comments."
- "You drink too much" vs. "I'm uncomfortable with your drinking."
- "You're angry and mean" vs. "I feel scared by your anger toward me."
- "You didn't care when I was upset" vs. "I felt hurt and unloved. I wanted you to show me you cared."
- "You were selfish to go with your friend" vs. "I felt as if you didn't care when you left."

Weigh your answers rather than blurting out your emotions (Prov. 15:28). If you want your husband to listen and understand how you feel, use "'I' statements." When you have to confront your husband with his behavior, focus directly on his actions by speaking the truth in love.

Admit Your Part in the Problem

Even when your husband is clearly in the wrong, your reactions and responses to his behavior can sometimes make the problem worse. Regardless of what he does, you're responsible for how you respond.

Prov. 15:1 says, "A gentle answer turns away wrath, but a harsh word stirs up anger." The Bible is full of verses that point out that the responsibility for our reaction to wrong-doing rests squarely on our own shoulders. I often lashed out at my husband in anger. I finally came to the place of owning my own behavior and learned to say, "I was un-comfortable with what you said to me, but my reaction to you was wrong. I'm sorry for what I said." Then I had to walk away. I could not *make* him acknowledge his part; that wasn't my purpose.

Rom. 12:18 says, "If it is possible, as far as it depends on you, live at peace with everyone." You're responsible for acknowledging your sins and offenses, regardless of what your husband does with his.

Jesus said, "The things that come out of the mouth come from the heart, and these make a man 'unclean'" (Matt. 15:18). God uses circumstances to show you what you need to change. Women in difficult marriages struggle with many destructive attitudes in their hearts: self-pity, self-righteousness, resentment, bitterness, anger, and many others. Being in a difficult marriage gives you an opportuni-ty to purify your heart. When you clean up your heart, your actions and reactions will fall in line.

Later I came to realize that I was self-righteous—judging my husband and looking upon him with contempt. Jesus said in Matt. 7:1-2, "Do not judge, or you too will be judged. For in the same way you judge others, you will be judged, and with the measure you use, it will be measured to you." Judging has to do with looking at people and pronouncing them guilty and condemning them. When you judge your husband, you're playing the role of God in his life. Jesus wants us to look inward and change ourselves first.

Check Your Motives

Changing yourself will require you to check your inner motives. Jesus was concerned with motives throughout the Sermon on the Mount (Matt. 5—7). He continually con-trasted outward behavior with what was going on in the heart. Was the motive behind praying or fasting to be seen by others? Then that didn't count with God. Hatred or lust hidden in the heart had the same root as murder and adultery as far as God was concerned. 1 Cor. 4:5 promises God "will bring to light what is hidden in darkness and will expose the motives of men's hearts."

Ask God to reveal the true motives of your heart, because "the heart is deceitful above all things and beyond cure" (Jer. 17:9). Becoming aware of your own motives allows you to take some of the focus off your husband. What is your motive when you answer your husband or confront him? Is it to be honest or hurtful? Are you saying no to him out of revenge or because it's not good for you to say yes? The reason prompting your action is often more important than your action. Here are some examples of right and wrong motives.

Right motives:
- To please God
- To do right
- To act in the best interest of the children
- To obey God
- To take responsibility for your actions
- To allow others to bear their own consequences
- To allow others to take care of their responsibilities
- To not enable
- To expose evil
- To be truthful
- To act out of love and compassion
- To be true to your beliefs and values
- To protect yourself and your children

Wrong motives:
- To punish and seek revenge
- To rescue (prevent someone from having to be responsible for his or her actions)
- To bear the consequences of another's behavior
- To manipulate and control

- To deceive or be dishonest
- To please someone else at the expense of hurting yourself or disobeying God
- To allow fear to dictate your choices

You may need to prioritize your motives. Tina and John separated when she found out about his affair. Tina was understandably angry with John, and she wondered if she should let him see the children. As long as there's no risk of emotional or physical damage to the children, she should let them go. If she refuses to let John see the children because she's angry and is seeking revenge, she would be making a decision based on wrong motives.

Jill's husband spends money irresponsibly. Jill is tired of going without things she wants because of his lack of responsibility and decides to spend money whether they can afford it or not. Jill's motive is wrong. If she decides to buy what she needs rather than sacrificing to make up for Lyle's irresponsibility, she would be making the decision out of a right motive.

Renee's husband, Sam, lost his driver's license due to driving under the influence of alcohol. Renee works four days a week. Sam expected Renee to change her work schedule and drive an hour out of her way each day to take him to and from work. If Renee wants to and could easily change her work schedule without resentment and consequence to her job, she could choose to do that. Or she could let Sam solve the problem on his own by courteously saying, "I'm not able to change my work schedule, but I could take you on my day off." She would be offering to take him when it worked for her without making extreme sacrifices. Sam would be left to suffer the natural consequences of his drinking. He could change his work schedule, find another ride, or take a bus. If Renee really wants to say no to Sam but didn't because she was afraid of his anger and displeasure, she's acting with a wrong motive.

Examine your motives and make sure they're right and pleasing to God. This can simplify many of the tough decisions you must make in your difficult marriage. Paul stated, "We are not trying to please men but God, who tests our hearts" (1 Thess. 2:4).

Adjust Your Expectations

Expectations are normal; everyone has them. It's reasonable to expect your husband to care, to listen, to carry his load of the household responsibilities, to control his addiction, to keep his word, to tell the truth, to show up when expected, to apologize when he's wrong, and to have compassion. The problem in difficult marriages is that many of these and other expectations are not fulfilled.

If you went to the hardware store expecting to buy a loaf of bread, you would be disappointed. Similarly, you're probably going to be disappointed if you expect your husband to do all the things "normal" husbands do. Just as it's futile to get angry with the clerk at the hardware store for not having bread, it's futile to be angry with your husband when he's unable to deliver normalcy in your relationship.

If you know your husband gets to drinking and fails to show up when expected, you're setting yourself up when you choose to wait for him. When you make your plans, take his frequent poor behavior into account. Does that make it all right? Of course not. But if you leave on time without him, at least you've not wasted energy being angry, and your evening is not completely ruined.

If your husband won't take out the trash, you can pout and fume, let the trash pile up, have a child take on the chore, or take the trash out with a good attitude. Know what is reasonable in your marriage, and exercise your power to choose what you do.

How many "my husband shoulds" are you living with? Any of the following?

● My husband should help around the house.

- My husband should pick up his own dirty clothes.
- My husband should be more social.
- My husband should go to men's Bible study.
- My husband should pray and lead family devotions.
- My husband should talk more.
- My husband should remember my birthday and our anniversary.
- My husband should bring me flowers.
- My husband should not get angry with me.
- My husband should make it possible for me not to have to work outside the home.
- My husband should do what he needs to do so I wouldn't have to deal with these problems.

If these or other "shoulds" are on your list and they aren't reasonable for your circumstances, let them go. Otherwise, you'll be disappointed and resentful. Solomon wrote that hope that's not fulfilled makes our hearts sick (Prov. 13:12). If your expectations are realistic, you'll spend less time being disappointed. Even in prison Paul was able to say, "I have learned to be content whatever the circumstances. I know what it is to be in need, and I know what it is to have plenty" (Phil. 4:11-12). Paul let go of expectations and accepted things the way they were.

Accept Him

Paul wrote in Rom. 15:7, "Accept one another, then, just as Christ accepted you, in order to bring praise to God."

Acceptance is an important part of being at peace with your life and the people in it. Your husband is who he is. If he struggles with anger and a hurtful past, then that's part of who he is. If your husband is an addict, he's an addict. No amount of wishing on your part will change that. When you accept that, you'll have more energy to put into controlling your responses, making good choices, taking care of yourself and your children, enjoying life, and exercising your options.

When you've accepted your husband for who he is, you can stop trying to change things over which you have no control and begin focusing on changing yourself and making the right choices for your life.

Approve of Him

Regardless of how difficult your husband is, you can find something in him to appreciate. Maybe he's good-looking, keeps a job, plays with the kids, is witty, fixes cars, is smart, works hard, helps around the house, supports your interests, or tries to stay sober. Whatever it is, notice it and compliment him for it.

Showing your approval will encourage your husband to do more things you can approve of. Your attitude could be a powerful motivator for him. Approval is like a gift; it softens the receiver's heart toward you (Prov. 18:16).

Use Your Influence

As a woman, you have the power to set the tone or mood of your home. "The wise woman builds her house, but with her own hands the foolish one tears hers down" (Prov. 14:1). How you respond to your husband will model the family's reaction to him. Regardless of his behavior, you still have a tremendous amount of influence for good or evil in your home. "Like a gold ring in a pig's snout is a beautiful woman who shows no discretion" (Prov. 11:22). Show your discretion by focusing on changing yourself.

Lifesaving Principle 4
Detach with Love

Choose for yourselves this day whom you will serve,
whether the gods your forefathers served beyond the River,
or the gods of the Amorites, in whose land you are living.
—Josh. 24:15

*W*ould you believe me if I told you that you could have a good life regardless of what your husband does?

Detachment is about separating yourself physically, emotionally, spiritually, and mentally from situations that affect you negatively. "A righteous man is cautious in friendship, but the way of the wicked leads them astray" (Prov. 12:26). A righteous woman in a difficult marriage is cautious in her relationship and guards her way by using detachment so that she's not led astray by poor choices her husband makes.

Detachment is about realizing that you're a separate person from your husband; you don't have to be affected by everything he says and does. You are responsible for your own feelings, thoughts, and actions, and your husband is responsible for his. This enables you to let him suffer the consequences of his choices and to take credit for his successes. If you can detach yourself from his behavior, you'll be able to *act* rather than constantly *react*. You can choose your behavior so that you do what's right, and you'll have fewer regrets. The choices you make can be good for you and pleasing to God.

Don't confuse loving detachment with abandonment.

You will still treat your husband with love and compassion, but you'll be free to live your own life with dignity.

God Detaches from Us

God allows us to make mistakes and even reject Him. But He loves us no matter what we do. He gives us boundaries, disciplines us, and permits us to suffer consequences but still gives us unconditional love. He doesn't always step in to rescue us but allows us to learn from our mistakes. He does not excuse our sins, yet He readily extends mercy and grace to us when we ask Him to.

When the woman caught in adultery came to Jesus, He looked at her with compassion but told her to stop sinning (John 8:2-11). He did not excuse or condone her sin but held her responsible for it and gave her a chance to change direction.

Model your loving detachment after God's.

It's His Problem

Your husband's problems are not your problems. "An evil man is snared by his own sin" (Prov. 29:6). "Each one is tempted when, by his own evil desire, he is dragged away and enticed. Then, after desire has conceived, it gives birth to sin" (James 1:14-15). Your husband is responsible for his drinking, sexual addiction, anger, drug use, or whatever he does. You cannot make him change his behavior, so why feel responsible for his choices? When you realize that his behavior is his choice, you can separate yourself from his decisions. You can "disengage" from his actions. That's the beginning of detachment.

It's your husband's responsibility to get the help he needs to change his behavior. *You* must focus on controlling *yourself* and *your* choices.

A Reason Is Not an Excuse

Your husband may have had a difficult childhood. Maybe he has a psychological problem or is unsaved and doesn't know any better. Frankly, that doesn't excuse him from responsibility for his behavior. God does not excuse sin.

Alcoholism is a disease—not because it can't be helped but because it can result in physical death. The addiction affects the body and grows progressively worse, much like other diseases. The alcoholic admits that he is powerless over the desire to drink once he starts drinking; however, he is fully responsible for taking the first drink and for the ways he hurts others when he drinks. The same principle applies to other problems. Your husband is responsible for choosing to do whatever it takes to make the situation better.

Knowing the reasons behind his behavior helps you feel compassion for him and helps you replace feelings of contempt with understanding. But you can still hold him accountable for his decisions. Don't confuse compassion with giving him an excuse to do anything he wants regardless of its effect on his family or others.

Give Up Enabling

Enablers make it possible for the alcoholic, addict, or abuser to continue negative behavior. If you're picking up the broken pieces, protecting your husband from consequences, covering up, taking over his responsibilities—you're enabling him. Enabling prevents change.

Enablers cover up irresponsibility for fear of losing financial or physical security. They keep the peace in the home so there will not be an upset. They make excuses to family and friends so no one will find out the truth. They make the children behave so there won't be a confrontation. They tolerate things that hurt because they're afraid of the consequences if they say no. They're afraid to speak the truth because they fear divorce. As a result, they actually prolong the problem.

The world works on natural principles that God has established. An apple falls to the ground because of gravity.

God established the law of reaping what we sow (Gal. 6:7-8). Wrong choices cause problems. Premarital sex may result in pregnancy or sexual disease. Drinking and driving can result in an accident and loss of your driver's license. Illegal drug use could result in jail time—that is, unless an enabler steps in and prevents the natural consequences from occurring.

An enabler can be a family member, a boss, or a friend. Perhaps the boss overlooks the errors his employee makes when he comes in hung over. A parent pays his grown child's bills when he or she refuses to work, or pays for legal bills when he or she is arrested for driving under the influence. A wife suffers in silence, too afraid to confront problems or admit them to outsiders. A mother weighs her every response to prevent her husband from getting angry in front of the children.

"If a man digs a pit, he will fall into it; if a man rolls a stone, it will roll back on him" (Prov. 26:27). If you're constantly catching your husband before he falls into the hole and holding on to the stone no matter the cost to yourself, you may be sabotaging your husband's best chance of getting well.

If you want to initiate change and improve your difficult marriage, it's essential that you stop enabling your husband. In the short run, things may get worse, but a good wife "brings him good, not harm, all the days of her life" (Prov. 31:12).

Detach from His Blame

In the Garden of Eden, Adam blamed God and Eve for his choice to eat the forbidden fruit. Eve blamed the serpent. Is your husband blaming you for his sin? "A man's own folly ruins his life, yet his heart rages against the Lord" (Prov. 19:3). Your husband may rage against you and blame you for his poor choices, but you can detach from it.

Do any of these blaming tactics sound familiar to you? "I wouldn't need pornography if you weren't so fat." "I wasn't going to drink tonight, but you were such a nag I had to get out of here." "You did that, so I have to do this. *You're* responsible for my choices." He shifts responsibility for his choices onto you, giving him an excuse for behavior he's planning to carry out anyway.

Maybe you aren't perfect. Maybe you do nag and get angry. Maybe you aren't the greatest housekeeper. But you still aren't responsible for his actions. The bottom line is this: Even when you do what he asks, he'll find something else to blame you for. And he'll continue to blame you as long as he wants to avoid responsibility.

In healthy marriages, spouses resolve conflicts by exploring the problems. A husband may say, "I'd like for the house to be more orderly. How could we work on that?" or "You seem upset tonight. I'm feeling nervous from work, and I'm having trouble dealing with you now, so I'm going to take some time to unwind. We can talk later if that's OK." This shows an ownership of feelings and needs without blame.

Here's the converse of that healthy scenario. You've had a hard day with the kids when your husband calls you, and you end up being a little short with him. So he comes home withdrawn, drunk, and angry. When you ask him what's wrong, he says, "You were rude to me on the phone." You try to apologize and explain, but he won't listen. He's unwilling to forgive, let it go, or hear your explanation. You think, *If only I hadn't gotten so uptight, the night would have been different.* In reality, his blame is a tool to manipulate you and shift to you the responsibility for his own choices and reactions.

Regardless of what you did and whether or not it was wrong, he has a choice about how he reacts and handles things. He has a responsibility to make good choices, and when he doesn't, it's his failure, not yours.

Detach from His Anger

Prov. 29:22 says, "An angry man stirs up dissension, and a hot-tempered one commits many sins." Prov. 22:24-25 says, "Do not make friends with a hot-tempered man, do not associate with one easily angered, or you may learn his ways and get yourself ensnared." When your husband is angry, don't argue or engage him. Walk away. Withhold your comment. Does that mean you passively stand there and take the anger without a word? No. Prov. 15:1 tells us that "A gentle answer turns away wrath, but a harsh word stirs up anger." You can answer gently, stating that you want to wait to discuss things with him when he's less angry. If he continues following you, leave the house. The goal is to protect yourself from his anger by refusing to argue. Prov. 20:3 says, "It is to a [person's] honor to avoid strife, but every fool is quick to quarrel."

Your husband's anger may not even be about the issue he's focusing on. He may be feeling insecure, unhappy with himself, upset about work, or is just wanting to control you. Don't assume that you caused his anger.

If he becomes violent, make alternate plans to ensure your safety. You must walk away from him when he's hurting you.

Detach from His Moods

Learn to separate yourself from his changing moods. Have you noticed that when he's uptight and anxious, so are you? When he's angry, are you angry? Are you in a better mood when he's happy? Do you decide how you feel when he walks in the door and you see how he's behaving?

It's OK for you to take the focus off him and put it on yourself and choose to have a good day even if he's having a bad one, to be happy even if he's unhappy. Pay attention to how you feel before you notice how he feels. Then choose to continue feeling that way.

Detach from His Threats

It's "better to meet a bear robbed of her cubs than a fool in his folly" (Prov. 17:12). If your husband does not hold himself accountable, he'll react strongly to anyone who confronts him. If he has threatened you, your natural tendency was probably to panic, taking his threats seriously. The purpose of his threats is to control you and get you to back down.

Angela's husband threatened divorce every time she set a firm boundary. She then backed down out of fear he might leave. Once she learned to detach, the next time he said he was thinking about leaving, she answered, "Maybe that's the right thing for you. Go if you need to." He didn't go. The important thing was that she stood her ground and was not controlled by his threat.

Difficult men know your fears and will use threats to leave to get control, especially when they sense change. Toby Rice Drews states in *Getting Them Sober: A Guide for Those Who Live with an Alcoholic* (South Plainfield, N.J.: Bridge Publishing, 1980), "Don't reveal your fears when he acts like he doesn't need you anymore. Remember you are dealing with a paper tiger" (84).

How many times has your husband threatened you and not done what he threatened? Did his threats convince you to back down and change your course of action? Did they make you question yourself? The answers to these questions will help you understand why he threatened you.

Detach from Crises

A crisis is any significant event that has a negative effect on your life, your husband's life, your marriage, or your children's lives. Your husband's losing his job or getting arrested or having your electricity turned off are examples of crises. "Stern discipline awaits him who leaves the path; he who hates correction will die" (Prov. 15:10). A crisis is

God's way of allowing your husband to be disciplined in the hope that he'll be saved.

Prov. 19:19 says, "A hot-tempered man must pay the penalty; if you rescue him, you will have to do it again." If your husband is hung over, don't call his boss and make an excuse. Let him handle it. Do not lecture, explain, or remind him.

If you jump in and prevent your husband from experiencing pain, you're prolonging that pain. If he doesn't pay the electric bill, don't pay it for him. Let him figure out how to have the electricity turned back on. In the meantime, stay somewhere else.

If he goes out to drink, don't stop him. But don't allow him to drive you or the children anywhere. You don't even have to be around him when he's intoxicated. If he gets in an accident, let him deal with the police, insurance, and car repairs.

On the other hand, it isn't your job to force a crisis to try to get his attention. That would be just as destructive as preventing a crisis. If you're mad at him because he spends too much money, don't purposefully spend the money that should be used to pay the electric bill. Don't go without food or necessities because he overspent. Take care of your responsibilities and yourself. Don't call his boss and tell him he has a drug problem, but don't lie for him when his boss calls to find out why he didn't come to work.

How do you survive a crisis? Take care of yourself and your children, and let your husband take care of himself. Do what you can, and let God take care of the rest.

Detach from His Family and Friends

You may be tempted to blame others for your husband's problems. Maybe his friends are a negative influence, or his boss puts undue stress on him. It's common to blame his parents for the way they raised him, or perhaps they enable him and make excuses for him. They may even deny he has a problem. Remember—your husband is a grown man and is responsible for his own behavior.

You can't change the people who influence your husband any more than you can change him. Treat them courteously, but don't allow them to mistreat you. You don't have to be around them more than necessary, and you don't have to solve their problems. You're not obligated to fix his relationships with them. We're warned not to be meddlers (1 Pet. 4:15).

Take Care of Your Responsibilities

Continue to do the things you're supposed to do with the right attitude. Neglecting your responsibilities is not appropriate detachment.

In every marriage there's a division of responsibilities. Whatever your agreed-upon responsibilities are, carry them out—even if he doesn't carry out his, even if he's in a bad mood. Carry them out with a cheerful attitude and to the best of your ability. If it's your responsibility to cook dinner, have it ready on time, even if he's late or doesn't come to the table. You can put the food away or leave it out. Either way, it's his responsibility to eat it. Take care of your part, and let him take care of his part. "Whatever you do, work at it with all your heart, as working for the Lord, not for men, since you know that you will receive an inheritance from the Lord as a reward" (Col. 3:23-24).

Be Courteous

A difficult marriage is fertile ground for sarcasm, snide remarks, silence, withdrawal, and bitterness. It's important that your tone of voice and interaction with your husband not communicate contempt, hostility, and disdain.

No matter how bad your marital relationship has become, common courtesy will change the tone in your home. "Let your conversation be always full of grace, seasoned with salt, so that you may know how to answer everyone" (Col. 4:6). If you've allowed your tone to become rude, demeaning, or unpleasant, learn to speak in a pleasant way, even when you don't feel like it. The expressions "Please," "Thank you," and "You're welcome" communicate respect and kindness. Do nice things for him to let him know you care. Offer to bring him a cup of water or a glass of tea. Offer to help when he's working around the house. Ask him to go with you to the mall or the park, even if you know he won't want to go. Give him the same courtesy you would give a friend or a guest. This is how you choose to love those who mistreat you (Rom. 12:20).

Step off the Eggshells

Do you tread lightly so as not to upset or displease your husband? Maybe you quickly clean the house before he gets home from work, or you tell your children to be good around him so he won't get mad. You may wait until he's in a good mood to discuss things or pretend you're in a good mood so he won't blow up. It's good to try to please your husband, but doing those things in an effort to control him is a guaranteed failure.

Walking on eggshells is sometimes done to manipulate others. If your motive is to influence your husband, you're starting with the premise that your actions determine his behavior. If you're going to do something nice for him, do it without expecting a payoff for yourself. Remember—you aren't responsible for him, so quit trying to be someone you're not, and be who you are. You'll like yourself better, and in the long run he might too.

Halley's husband doesn't like spending holidays with her family. He goes, but he always appears sullen and withdrawn and insists on leaving early. She dutifully leaves when he says he's ready to go. Then she gets mad at him and accuses him of ruining her holiday. When she finally started to understand detachment, she told him nicely that she understood his feelings about holidays, so she would take the second car in case he wanted to leave early. She was able to relax and enjoy her evening. That's how detachment works.

Don't Argue with the Problem

When your husband is under the influence of alcohol or drugs, in a "dry drunk," raging, behaving irrationally, or in a bad mood, don't argue with him. "A fool finds no pleasure in understanding but delights in airing his own opinions" (Prov. 18:2). Fools refuse to be reproved. Prov. 23:9 says, "Do not speak to a fool, for he will scorn the wisdom of your words."

There will be a time to speak to him. As Prov. 26:5 says, "Answer a fool according to his folly, or he will be wise in his own eyes." However, that time is not when he's in an unreasonable state. Instead of arguing or trying to convince him when he's drunk that he needs help, try talking to him when he wakes up with a hangover. Instead of talking to him when he's angry, talk to him after he's calmed down. Use wisdom to determine when you should speak.

Here are some practical ways to respond to your husband when he's in the mood to argue.

- "No."
- "Yes."
- "Maybe."
- "You could be right."
- "I'll think about that."
- "Could be."
- "Thank you."
- "I hear you."
- "I understand."
- "That's your opinion."
- "I might."
- "Possibly."
- "Good point."

Do you notice similarities in these answers? They're all short. They end the conversation in a gracious way. They're not open to argument. They prevent you from saying something you don't mean. They prevent you from responding in anger. They distance you from your husband's words and anger. In other words, they all help you detach rather than allow you to be hooked into an argument.

If your husband won't stop when you walk away, and he follows you, you can simply say, "I don't want to talk right now." You can even leave the house for a time if necessary.

Don't Believe Lies

Your husband may try to dupe you into accepting responsibility for his bad behavior by saying that you're causing the problems. He may tell you that you're a bad cook, that you're mean to him, that you say the wrong things, that you're a bad mom, that you're a terrible housekeeper, that you're too fat, and so on. His hurtful comments may come from his need to blame you for his problems, from his own insecurity, or from his need to control you. Even though what he says hurts you, you can choose whether or not you want to believe him.

Remember—it's his problem talking. Don't let his words have too much power over you. You don't have to accept his words as the truth, and you must not let his words destroy you. You can choose not to take his comments personally. "Like a fluttering sparrow or a darting swallow, an undeserved curse does not come to rest" (Prov. 26:2).

Don't Let Him Push Your Buttons

It may be an attitude, an action, a look, a response, or a subject—anything you have a strong reaction to every time. It may be a phrase he uses, or he may deliberately ignore something that's important to you. Regardless of what it is, you'll know it's your button, because you'll sense an instant reaction in yourself. "Pushing your buttons" can be anything that's intentionally used to irritate you.

Why does your husband push your buttons? So you'll react and he can use your reaction as an excuse to blame you for his behavior. When you detach, he may increase his attempts to make you react (as you used to)—so be prepared.

Live Your Life

You can help yourself stop being obsessed with what he's doing, thinking, and feeling by focusing on what you're doing at that moment. Keep yourself busy doing the things you need to do. Matt. 6:34 reminds us to focus on what we need to do today.

Keeping your thoughts on what you're doing at the moment is a powerful way to put detachment into practice. At the end of the day, you'll have accomplished what you need to do, and you'll feel good about yourself and your life.

Act As If

Detachment takes practice. At first you may catch yourself falling into old habits, and you may feel paralyzed with fear when you let him suffer the consequences of his actions. You may feel that you betrayed him when you let him fall. It might not seem right when you attend a function without him because he didn't come home in time. That's OK. Do it anyway.

"Acting as if" is when you choose how you're going to act even if you don't really feel like it. You act detached by doing things that show you're detached. Eventually you'll begin to *feel* the independence that comes from detachment.

You've probably talked your way into oblivion trying to get him to straighten up. Face it—he's tuned you out. He'll notice a change in your actions before he hears anything else you have to say.

Detach with Love

When you detach from your husband with love, you're allowing him to be an adult and make his own decisions without you overseeing them and trying to control them.

See your husband as he is: an imperfect human struggling with a problem that's overtaking him. He may be doing the best he knows how to do, and you can still have compassion for his struggles. See him not as an evil man bent on destroying you but as a hurting child of God who needs help. This will allow you to replace hatred and contempt with kindness and courtesy. "Do not repay evil with evil" when he mistreats you or return his "insult with insult" (1 Pet. 3:9). Do not retaliate. You can literally bring him a cup of water and treat him with dignity even when he's mistreating you (Prov. 25:21-22).

Even though you feel compassion, don't excuse his behavior, and don't allow yourself to be used and mistreated. See him as an adult who's responsible for his choices and who needs to suffer the natural consequences of his choices. "In the paths of the wicked lie thorns and snares, but he who guards his soul stays far from them" (Prov. 22:5). Detachment guards your soul. It's part of taking care of yourself.

Lifesaving Principle 5

Nurture Yourself

After all, no one ever hated his own body,
but he feeds and cares for it, just as Christ does the church.
—Eph. 5:29

Do you use any of these excuses for not taking care of yourself?

- "I don't have the time."
- "I don't have the money."
- "I'm too overwhelmed with my problems."
- "I don't have fun anyway."
- "I don't do things that make my husband angry."
- "I don't want to be selfish."

In order to deal with the demands placed on you, you must learn to take care of yourself. On airplanes they tell the mothers to put on their oxygen masks first—then take care of their children. If you don't stabilize yourself first, you'll not be able to help others around you.

Taking care of yourself is not something you do *instead of* taking care of your family. It's about learning to nurture and revitalize yourself the right way. It's about valuing yourself as God intended you to.

The Prov. 31 woman had many interests and talents that she cultivated while caring for her family: She shopped, sewed, invested, cooked, worked for charities, ran a business, and taught. She was a mother, friend, businesswoman, wife, charity worker, employer, and civic leader. And in everything she did she was clothed with strength, dignity, and confidence.

You may have pushed your own needs aside for so long that you don't even know what interests you anymore. Ask yourself these questions:

- What did I like to do before I married?
- What do I find myself dreaming about?
- What do I regret not doing?
- What do I envy about other women?
- What things motivate and interest me?
- If I could do anything I want, what would it be?
- What motivates me to action?
- What relaxes me?
- What looks like fun when I see others doing it?

Your answers might give you a few ideas of things that will help you relax, grow your talents, improve your self-esteem, and feel better about your life.

It's Not Selfish

Jesus said to love others as you love yourself (Matt. 22:39). He understands that if you don't value yourself, you'll be of little help to others. Motivated by compassion for those in need, Jesus extended himself, but there came a time when He would go away to rest, pray, and recuperate (Matt. 14:13, 23). You can learn to do the same. The more stressful your life is, the more rebuilding you need.

Your husband may not like it much when you begin to take care of yourself. Addicts and other dysfunctional people are self-centered, and he may accuse you of being selfish. As stated previously, Prov. 18:2 tells us, "A fool finds no pleasure in understanding but delights in airing his own opinions." You can let your husband express his feelings, but don't let him dissuade you from doing something that's good for you. Nurturing yourself helps you become a healthier person—and that's good for your marriage, even if your husband feels uncomfortable.

Take Care of Your Emotional Needs

Don't overlook taking care of your own emotional needs. Find someone who knows your situation, listens to you, and can help you see things clearly. It should be someone who's emotionally and spiritually mature and who's experienced similar problems. She must be willing to tell you the truth even when it hurts.

Girlfriends are important. Who else understands menopause, hormones, and PMS? Even if your marriage were healthy, your husband can't meet all your emotional and relational needs. It will take some of the pressure off your relationship with your husband if you have friends.

Learning to avoid emotional overreactions is an important way for you to take care of yourself. I had a habit of escalating arguments by arguing and refusing to drop a subject until I felt it was resolved. After a big confrontation, I felt emotionally drained and mentally, spiritually, and physically exhausted. Plus I had a big mess to clean up: apologies, regrets, embarrassment, and guilt. I had to learn to do whatever it took to keep me from reacting with emotional extremes. Be aware of your emotional vulnerability. "He who guards his lips guards his life, but he who speaks rashly will come to ruin" (Prov. 13:3).

Take Care of Your Physical Needs

God created you to need rest and rejuvenation. Physical depletion prevents you from handling your emotions well and responding competently to problems.

It's also easy to be resentful toward others when you're overextended. Kaitlin felt angry toward her husband for watching Monday night football when she was running around trying to cook, clean up the kitchen, and take care of the house and kids. She finally decided to buy pizza on Mondays and watch the game with him. Remember—you need recreation too.

Try to get regular exercise. I've taken a walk every day for more than 15 years. Praying and quieting my mind while walking helps me let go of stress. This activity is a priority because I know I don't function well without it.

Pay attention to your diet. Eating right helps with weight control and gives you more energy. Skipping meals decreases your energy and your ability to think clearly. Most women need a daily vitamin supplement in addition to a healthy diet.

If you suspect there's a cyclical pattern of some sort to irritability or feeling depressed, keep a calendar of your physical and emotional symptoms. There's no need to let hormonal problems from premenstrual syndrome, peri-menopause, or menopause rob you of a feeling of well-being. See your doctor to discuss your nutritional, physical, and hormonal needs.

Although prescription drugs should not be used as a substitute for dealing with your problems, there are times when antidepressants or tranquilizers are necessary. Severe depression and anxiety sometimes require medication to be corrected. Talk to your doctor.

When you're worn down physically or mentally, it's not the time to take on a big project, make a major decision, or initiate a long, serious talk with your husband.

Don't neglect your appearance. Put on makeup every day. Keep your hair clean and styled. Indulge yourself. Doing little things to improve your appearance will give your self-esteem a boost.

Don't ignore your own needs. You will find it's easier to stand up for yourself when you're feeling confident.

Take Care of Your Spiritual Needs

There were times when I felt like a hypocrite in church until I understood that the weaker I was the nearer God was to me. As Ps. 34:18 says, "The LORD is close to the brokenhearted and saves those who are crushed in spirit." Jesus said He came to call sinners—not the righteous—to repentance (Matt. 9:13). I wondered if God really wanted to hear my worship when I had so much ugliness in my marriage and my heart. I learned to offer a sacrifice of praise in spite of how I felt.

If you're so spent emotionally that you have difficulty reading the Bible, try reading a good devotional book or just the Psalms and Proverbs. The Psalms will bring you comfort in the midst of your struggle, and Proverbs is full of common sense and wisdom in one-verse nuggets. Read the Bible for its general truth, but don't try to personalize every verse. Taking every scripture literally as God's specific promise or warning when you're in a state of confusion can result in misinterpreting what you read. Just try reading it consistently; it's better to meditate on a single verse each day than to read 10 chapters once a week. Reading the Bible helps you grow in wisdom and knowledge, something you definitely need in a difficult marriage.

Heb. 10:25 tells of the importance of meeting with other Christians to encourage each other. Do something that connects you to other Christians. Consider joining a women's Bible study, reading a Christian book, or listening to Christian radio. Praise music can also be very healing when you're feeling discouraged and confused.

If you're feeling discouraged because it seems that your prayers are unanswered, use your prayer time to talk to God about what's going on in your life. Prayer deepens your relationship with God, aligns your will to His, reduces anxiety, and helps you to trust Him. Ask Him for wisdom, discernment, guidance, and strength. Simple prayers count too: *Help me. Guide me. Give me Your strength. Keep me from sin. Forgive me. Thank You. Your will, not mine.*

Take Care of Your Mental Needs

You can take care of your mental needs by following current events, reading books, volunteering, getting a part-time job, taking a college or adult education course, or learning a new craft or skill. You may find that you're a better wife and mother when you expand your knowledge and interests.

Use Your Talents

Even though you already feel overwhelmed, helping others is good for you. There are many areas you can help in: teaching Sunday School; working in the nursery; volunteering in community and charitable organizations such as a nursing home, unwed mothers' home, or homeless shelter; or helping a friend, family member, neighbor, or coworker in time of need. It can be little things such as giving someone a ride, fixing soup for someone who's sick, offering encouragement, sharing a good tape or book, or listening to someone else's problems. It may even be listening to another woman in a difficult marriage and giving her encouragement and wisdom from your experiences. The Prov. 31 woman extended her arms to the needy (v. 20).

Helping others balances your concerns and keeps you from being too self-centered. You're responsible for what you do with your life and talents (Matt. 25:14-30) including your insight, experience, and opportunities. Instead of putting off using your talents until after your marriage problems are resolved, use them fully today.

Julie wanted to teach Sunday School but put off volunteering to do so because Ed didn't always want her to go to church. Once she made the commitment, to her surprise, he accepted it after a short time, and she loved it. She met other Christians and found she was a great teacher.

Have Some Fun

Treat yourself to relaxation and fun. It doesn't have to be an expensive vacation. Learn to do little activities: take a walk in the park, see a play, enjoy lunch with a friend, have your nails done or get a massage, sip a cup of coffee or tea, read a fun novel, take a bubble bath, go shopping, visit the beach or park, ride your bicycle, or do anything else that's fun for you. Do things with your children: play ball, swing, color a picture, or build a sand castle. At first you may be focused on your husband or feeling guilty, but before you know it you'll be having fun and liking it!

Solomon came to the conclusion that God wanted us to enjoy life, calling it "a gift of God" when we're able to find satisfaction (Eccles. 5:18-20).

Say No and Yes

Do you say yes when you really want to say no? Learn to be truthful and say no—especially when saying yes will leave you feeling resentful and angry. Jesus said to "simply let your 'Yes' be 'Yes,' and your 'No,' 'No'" (Matt. 5:37). Conversely, if you really want to do something, don't decline just to please someone else.

Accept your husband's gifts—flowers, dinner invitations, candy, or whatever else—as long as you can take care of yourself in the process. Don't shut the door on an opportunity for him to do something nice for you the best way he knows how. Accepting his gifts does not mean you approve of everything he does, nor does it mean you owe him anything.

Forgive Others

No doubt there are many unresolved conflicts and hurts that could easily fester into resentment in your marriage. Peter asked Jesus how many times he had to forgive, and Jesus essentially said there was no limit (Matt. 18:22).

Jesus told us that if we don't forgive, God won't forgive us (Matt. 6:15). In addition, a root of bitterness causes problems in all areas of your life.

Forgiveness does not mean you shouldn't take steps to prevent being hurt again. It's entirely appropriate to follow through with consequences even though you forgive. God allows us to suffer consequences even though He forgives us. Your distrust, emotional distance, and protective decisions are the result of your husband's behavior and part of his consequences. If he has lied to you, it's reasonable for you to distrust him and set up appropriate safeguards for yourself. If he's angry and abusive toward you, you'll naturally be distanced from him.

Make Good Decisions

Reaching a decision about anything can be complicated if you're in a difficult marriage. You often distrust your perceptions, opinions, and decision-making abilities, especially since many decisions have unpleasant consequences. Telling your husband no will be much harder for you than for a woman in a healthy marriage, since he's more likely to get angry and retaliate.

Nicole fears her husband's reaction to any decision she makes. Because he's so unpredictable, she never knows whether he'll overlook it or become angry and verbally abusive. She is trying to learn to make necessary decisions without letting the fear interfere.

Don't make decisions when you're angry or in the middle of a crisis. Wait until things have calmed down, since decisions made in the midst of crises often turn out to be empty threats. Talk through your decisions with other people, but remember that you're the one who has to do what your heart and conscience tell you, and you're the one who will be living with the outcome.

Let Go of Regrets

You carry a heavy load. That load can be made even heavier if you have unrealistic expectations about yourself. Do you feel you should be able to handle things better, change your husband, bear the pain courageously, keep everything running smoothly, and fix your marriage?

Maybe you tell yourself that you should have known better. You may be embarrassed or disappointed that you backed down from a boundary or believed his lies one more time. Perhaps you regret marrying him, staying with him, putting up with too much, or overreacting.

I struggled with these feelings. I came to understand that, although I could have had stronger boundaries earlier, my reasons for staying were good: I wanted to hold my marriage together, protect my children from the trauma of divorce, and obey God.

Guilt can be positive if it motivates you to change your behavior. The purpose of guilt is to let you know you made a mistake so that you'll repent (2 Cor. 7:10).

David said, "My guilt has overwhelmed me like a burden too heavy to bear" (Ps. 38:4). The Holy Spirit works through your conscience to convict you of sin. If you're not being convicted, something is wrong. God promises that He'll discipline you if you're His child (Heb. 12).

Jeanette frequently lost her temper with her children. Through her attendance of a weekly women's Bible study, she began to feel convicted. "I excused it before, as everyone in my family got angry easily," she said. "I know it's wrong, and I need to work on changing it." She was feeling constructive guilt.

On the other hand, if you feel guilty about *everything*, you'll have more difficulty discerning which feelings are convictions from the Holy Spirit versus your overly critical conscience.

Shame is different than guilt. Shame evokes feelings of worthlessness. If you feel that you're a mistake, a loser, no good, and incapable of doing anything right, recognize this as shame. God does not want you to feel this way. He let His Son die for you on the Cross. That act testifies to the fact that you are valuable in His eyes and worthy of being redeemed. Allow yourself to admit your mistakes—without feeling that you *are* a mistake.

Laura experienced verbal and sexual abuse as a child from her alcoholic stepfather. Her husband is also an alcoholic and verbally abusive. Feeling that everything she does is wrong, she says, "No wonder Ted doesn't love me—I'm a loser. No one could possibly love me. He's right—I can't do anything right. I can't even cook dinner without burning it." Laura is experiencing shame. Rather than just knowing she made a mistake by burning dinner, she feels worthless.

Saul murdered Christians, yet God redeemed him, changed his name to Paul, and used him mightily for His kingdom. God never reminded him of his past. Paul let go of his past by living for God in the present (Acts 9:1-9; Gal. 1:13).

Regardless of how you have lived in your difficult marriage in the past, try to accept the fact that you did the best you could at the time. "God's kindness leads you toward repentance" (Rom. 2:4)—not His harsh judgment. Since God forgives you, forgive yourself.

Honest reflection and an acceptance of your mistakes are important, but have grace and mercy toward yourself, a portion of the same grace and mercy God has toward you.

You can let go of your regrets by doing the following things:

- Acknowledge your mistakes.
- Believe you did the best you could at the time.
- Look for the good in your past.
- Accept the fact that you can't change the past.
- Accept God's forgiveness.
- Forgive yourself.
- Make changes in your life today so you don't repeat the mistakes.
- Expect God to redeem your past and use it for His glory.
- Look for ways to comfort and encourage others with the things you've learned.
- Expect God to work in your children's and husband's lives as He has worked in yours.

Try to treat yourself with the same compassion and mercy Jesus extended to the Samaritan woman (John 4:7-26). No mistake is ever wasted if you grow from it.

Keep a Journal

Journaling can help you gain a better perspective. It can help you let go of your past, grow in understanding of your present circumstances, and clarify confusing issues. It can also help you recognize patterns in your behavior and your husband's actions such as verbal abuse, reoccurring arguments, and triggers. It can also be a record of significant turning points or events in your relationship. Writing down important events, conversations, and insights helps validate your perceptions. When I doubted my feelings and perceptions, I wrote out my thoughts and fears and then countered them on paper with truth and God's promises.

Journaling can be used as a measuring stick of your growth or lack of growth. Write insights about your life, marriage, and relationship with the Lord. Keeping notes of things God is teaching you and writing lists of things you're thankful for help you focus on your relationship with Him.

Francine started journaling whenever she felt really confused or upset. Looking back months later, she was surprised at how often her husband got angry with her when she did anything independent of him. She also noted that he always accused her of being unkind to him before he went to the bars. Seeing this pattern helped her realize that he used her as an excuse to drink and that he was threatened by her independence. She is less affected by his disapproval when she knows she didn't do anything wrong.

Watch Priorities

It can be hard to keep up with life, even without marriage problems. Determining your priorities will help you prevent feeling overwhelmed. Try writing a list of everything you need to do and number them in order of importance. Items with deadlines come first, as well as things your children need, such as help with homework.

Accept the fact that you may not be able to do everything on the list. Do what you can, and let the rest go; the urgent things are not always the most important. Housework can usually wait, and errands can often be put off. Spending necessary time with family is usually something that does not feel urgent but is very high in importance.

If you have trouble taking care of yourself physically, emotionally, mentally, and spiritually, put those things on your list too.

Jesus warned the religious leaders of His day that they were paying too much attention to unimportant things while neglecting "the more important matters of the law—justice, mercy and faithfulness" (Matt. 23:23). Doing things that lead to righteousness is always a priority (Matt. 6:33).

Keep It Simple

Life can be complicated. My dad shared an important observation of life with me. He told me that each year of my life I would add a little more. First it would be getting married, then having one child, then buying a house, then having another child, then a dog, and so on. He said we gradually adjust to doing more, but if we added it all at once, we could never handle it!

In order to counter the tendency to add more to your life, you have to choose to keep it simple by deliberately taking the simple way rather than the complicated way—especially when you're feeling overwhelmed. It can mean fixing an easy dinner instead of a four-course meal, buying a gift certificate rather than shopping for a gift, having a small party instead of a large one, wearing clothes that are easy to wash and maintain (that means no ironing), or having a child's party at the skating rink where it's all done for you. Your motive is not to be lazy—it's to take care of yourself so your life stays manageable.

Respect Yourself

Treat yourself with respect, and know you deserve to be treated respectfully by the people in your life. Children will respect you more when you don't accept disrespectful treatment from them or your husband. Your husband may treat you better when you expect to be valued. You'll receive more honor when you're "clothed with strength and dignity" (Prov. 31:25). You'll hear, "Give her the reward she has earned, and let her works bring her praise at the city gate" (Prov. 31:31). Nurturing yourself is how you treat yourself with respect. It's an important part of improving your life.

Lifesaving Principle

Face Your Fears

6

When I am afraid, I will trust in you.
—Ps. 56:3

Do you ask yourself any of the following questions?
What if he leaves?
What if he does it again?
What if he gets angry?
What if he has an affair?
What if he gets hurt or hurts someone else?
What if he loses his job?
What if he doesn't come home?
What if we lose the house?
What if the kids find out?
What if I get sick?
What if he gets arrested?
What if we can't pay the bills?
What if I can't make it on my own?
Whether the threat is real or not, the fear you feel is very real. In fact, fear is probably the primary underlying emotion that governs many of your decisions.

Fear can either motivate you or paralyze you. Fear is what moves you to get out of the way of a train or bus or sends you to the doctor when you feel a suspicious lump. It can also keep you from telling your husband the truth, asking for help, and making changes in yourself and your life.

Anxiety is a state of mind that causes one to focus on future events with an associated feeling of fear. It weighs you down and results in associated nervousness manifested by butterflies in your stomach, edginess, irritability, and the inability to cope, make decisions, concentrate, and sleep.

Fear Is Not a Sin

Fear can lead you to depend on God, but it can also lead you away from Him. Jesus repeatedly directed the disciples to turn their fear into faith by trusting Him rather than reacting with worry and anxiety (See Matt. 14:22-32; John 6:16-21; Luke 8:22-25; Phil. 4:6).

Consider these examples: Your husband is drinking beer and driving his motorcycle. You have a lump in your breast the doctor calls suspicious. Your husband tells you he's considering filing for divorce. Your son has been called up to active duty. It's normal for these circumstances to produce fear.

What are you going to do with that fear? You can project into the future and fall apart, or you can face it and choose to give your fears to God. Lisa Beamer, Todd Beamer's wife, pregnant with her third child, was able to completely trust the Lord after Todd's death on Flight 963, the plane that crashed near Somerset, Pennsylvania, on September 11, 2001. She had fear and anxiety about her future but chose to trust God with the outcome.

Specific Fears

As you read through these common fears, try to identify the ones that affect your decisions and actions. Once you identify your fears, you'll be better equipped to deal with them and prevent them from affecting your decisions and ruling your life.

Fear of Your Husband's Reaction

Every time she opens her mouth to speak, Hannah worries about what John's reaction will be. Sometimes he's pleasant and reasonable, but at other times he rages and berates her. She constantly watches him to gauge his mood and then decides whether or not she'll talk to him. She's even more anxious when they're with other people, because she never knows how he'll react to what she says. Sometimes it's not worth going out, because she feels so nervous the whole time.

1 John 4:18 says that "fear has to do with punishment." God says, "Do not fear the reproach of men or be terrified by their insults" (Isa. 51:7). Can you see how this fear could rule your life? You can't live up to your values and standards or follow your own conscience if you let fear of your husband's reactions direct your steps rather than allowing God to guide you.

Fear of Change

When you think of change, do you feel anger, panic, loss of control, sadness, or hopelessness? If you experience these or similar feelings, you fear change.

Marita felt overwhelmed at the prospect of changing jobs. Even thinking of the new situations she would face caused her to lose sleep and experience anxiety attacks. But that was nothing compared to her fears about the changes that would occur in her life if she and Joel didn't make it. Just the thought of starting over on her own panicked her. She decided that she would put up with anything to hold her marriage together.

God can't change you or your marriage if you desperately try to keep things the same because you're afraid. Ps. 112:7 says, "He will have no fear of bad news; his heart is steadfast, trusting in the Lord." God's counsel to you is "have no fear of sudden disaster or of the ruin that overtakes the wicked, for the Lord will be your confidence and will keep your foot from being snared" (Prov. 3:25-26). God does not want you to fear change.

Fear of Loss

You can determine what your true priorities are by

thinking about what you fear losing most. I realized that I feared losing my house and lifestyle more than I feared losing more important things like peace in my home and a stable and consistent environment in which to raise my daughters. I also underestimated the loss of my dignity, self-esteem, and respect. Prov. 15:16-17 says, "Better a little with the fear of the LORD than great wealth with turmoil. Better a meal of vegetables where there is love than a fattened calf with hatred." Consider all you're giving up, and make sure your priorities are right.

You may realistically fear the loss of your husband's life, driver's license, job, health, or sobriety. Even if in your situation the possibility of one or more of those things happening is real, you can't live today as though it were actually happening—especially since you have no control. Decide to face the loss if and when it happens, not before, because the day may never come. In Matt. 6:25-34, Jesus said not to worry about material things: food, clothes, money, and even our lives. He asked, "Who of you by worrying can add a single hour to his life?" (v. 27).

God knows what it's going to take to change your husband. Some loss may be necessary to make him willing to change. If you fear that loss so much that you prevent it, you may actually be getting in God's way. Many addicts have been miraculously spared injury in an accident that has been their turning point. Others have been injured or injured others and faced the seriousness of their problem from a hospital bed or a jail cell.

Sharon says, "I have frantically kept everything together out of fear of losing our house and lifestyle. I did whatever it took to make sure Jeff got to work, paid the bills, and didn't drive when he was drunk. I even went with him sometimes so I could drive him home. I've come to the conclusion that if we lose the house it will be hard, but I can't keep all these balls in the air. I have to let him face his own consequences. I'm convinced God wants me to do what's right and to trust Him."

Leah says, "I have more peace in my apartment alone than I had in that big house with Rudy. I won't say it was easy going back to work and losing my home and marriage, but I would rather have peace in an apartment than all the anger and turmoil I tolerated. In retrospect, that was much harder."

Don't let the loss of anything be more important to you than standing for what's right and pleasing to the Lord. Losing material things or being on your own is hard. Even though the prospect seems overwhelming, you can't let the fear of loss keep you from doing what is right.

Fear of Divorce

There is no doubt that divorce seems like the ultimate threat and the hallmark of failure. Even if you know you can survive financially, you may not feel that you can survive emotionally. Your self-esteem may be low and your self-doubt high.

Divorce is difficult. However, the fear of divorce can keep you imprisoned in a difficult marriage. If divorce is the ultimate threat, then you'll find yourself backing down from stating your truth, setting boundaries, and taking a stand for right whenever you feel that your actions could result in a divorce.

Your husband may know you fear divorce and use it to get you to back down when you make changes that are uncomfortable for him.

Sue complains to John that she's not sure how much longer she can live with his drinking and his angry outbursts toward her and the children. She's really letting John know how she feels and is asking him to get help. She's not asking for a divorce, and John knows that. But John doesn't want to change. He senses a new resolve in Sue, and although it scares him, his response to her doesn't reveal that. Instead, he says, "If you don't like it, leave.

There's the door. I can live without you." Sue feels devastated, discounted, and ignored, but mostly afraid. So she drops the issue for a while. Mission accomplished. John prevented Sue from changing. Until Sue understands that John is probably at least as afraid or more afraid of losing her than she is of losing him, John will continue to use this as a ploy to control her and prevent change.

If your husband really thinks divorce is imminent or no big deal, why doesn't he do it? When he threatens divorce, what is the effect on you? Do you shrink back, thinking if you tell him more about the way you feel he will leave you? If so, he's controlling your behavior and preventing you from confronting him.

As a Christian, you probably feel strongly that God does not want you to divorce. Yet if you're held captive by the fear of divorce, you're a prisoner. It may be necessary to risk losing a bad relationship to gain a good one. If you never tell your husband that he has crossed a line and may lose his marriage, you're ultimately powerless. If you stand for what's right and your husband chooses to leave, then it's his choice and not yours (1 Cor. 7:15). If you're completely unable to provide for your needs on your own and have no one to turn to for help, it would be prudent for you to begin to get some type of job skills. Making provision will give you increased security and reduce your fears.

Fear of Being Alone

You're carrying enormous loads now and making it. You may be handling a job, kids, daily turmoil, and uncertainty in addition to your marriage problems—and without the support of your husband. The truth is that most women in difficult marriages are very capable women with enormous survival skills, and you may very well be *emotionally* alone in your marriage already. You're a capable adult with the ability to make it on your own if need be, especially with God's promises and provisions.

God says to you "'Do not be afraid; you will not suffer shame. Do not fear disgrace; you will not be humiliated. . . . For your Maker is your husband—the Lord Almighty is his name. . . . The Lord will call you back as if you were a wife deserted and distressed in spirit—a wife who married young, only to be rejected'" (Isa. 54:4-6). You're not really alone when you have the Lord.

Fear of Disappointment

Your husband makes another promise: "I won't _____ again." You've heard it many times. Addicts often promise to change, and your husband may mean it. Then again, it may just be a way to get you off his back. Accept the reality that he may fall, but don't let that possibility control you.

When he's ready to change, he'll be ready to do whatever it takes. He'll go to a program, get counseling, change his attitude toward you, repent, and be broken. Lasting change is the result of hard work. Yet even then, people sometimes stop growing and slip back into old behaviors. You must honestly face that risk as you contemplate your future with him.

Maybe you're on the verge of separation or divorce. If you give him another chance, will he do it again? Maybe. Does staying with him put your life at risk of the possibility of a sexually transmitted disease? Are you leaving yourself vulnerable financially, emotionally, or physically? Assess your risk, protect yourself, and maintain firm boundaries.

It's important that you know you'll be OK and will be able to deal with it if he fails. The fear of disappointment is hard to overcome, as it requires you to really let go and put your hope in God and not your husband. As David said, "But now, Lord, what do I look for? My hope is in you" (Ps. 39:7).

Fear of Suicide

If your husband threatens suicide, he may be serious, or he may be using your fear as a way to control you. Joan noticed that when she began to get independent, Neal talked about how he was depressed and had nothing to live for. Feeling guilty for leaving him alone, she dropped her plans. She later realized that he was manipulating her and refused to give in.

If your husband is truly suicidal, you're not responsible for his decision to commit suicide. You can try to get help from family, friends, the police, a counselor, or a minister, always remembering that in the end his choices are beyond your control. (If a child talks about suicide or you have suicidal thoughts, get help.)

Fear of Feeling Your Emotions

Joyce didn't feel anger toward Bruce for the first five years of her marriage. "I stuffed my feelings when he put me down in front of other people so I didn't make it worse by creating a scene. Now, five years later, I'm beginning to feel angry about the emotional and verbal abuse. Some days I feel so angry that I want to throw him out. Other days, I feel incredibly sad and scared. I didn't know I had all these feelings because I did such a good job of pretending everything was OK."

You will feel—or may already have experienced—the sadness associated with your losses. You need to grieve over your unfulfilled dreams and hopes in order to accept the truth about your life.

The apostle Paul felt despair over all the trials he endured building the Early Church but concluded that all those things happened to bring him to the place where he could fully rely on God (2 Cor. 1:8). Your feelings should not be ignored, but they don't have to control your life.

Don't fall into the trap of believing that your thoughts and feelings, or those of others, are premonitions. I remember a time when I was apprehensive about flying. A friend said to me, "Don't go. I don't feel good about your trip." It unnerved me, but in the end I reasoned that it was her fear and not a sign from God. I went, and the trip was fine.

God speaks through the Bible, people, circumstances, and open doors. Don't give prophetic status to every thought that pops into your head. Instead, you're to control your thoughts and your fears, taking them captive and making them "obedient to Christ" (2 Cor. 10:5).

Fear of Being out of God's Will

There are different ways to determine God's will for your life. I started searching for God's perfect will for my life as a teenager. I attended a church that stressed hearing God's voice, and I waited for God to clearly speak to me regarding my career. When I didn't hear His voice, I was disillusioned for a few years.

God rarely speaks directly to us. If we wait to hear "a voice," we'll be frustrated or tempted to follow after thoughts and whims, mistakenly attributing them to the Holy Spirit speaking to us. That is not to say that God doesn't use the Holy Spirit to speak to us by impressions or thoughts, but we must always use discernment and have confirmation from other sources, and we should never assume that God *has* to direct us in those ways.

Whatever we do, our decisions should never conflict with the Bible. We're also told to "make plans by seeking advice" (Prov. 20:18). God directs by opening and shutting doors or opportunities (as He did for Paul with ministry opportunities as mentioned in 2 Cor. 2:12). If God wants you to do something, He'll provide a way for you to do it. Pray about your decisions, seek advice through the Bible and others, and then use wisdom to make a choice.

Martha waits to feel God's guidance for even small decisions. She's always waiting for some sign: a thought, a Scripture, or something she hears. When one of her decisions turns out to be wrong, she wonders why God misled her. Martha has a misconstrued idea of how to seek God's will.

If you're a Christian who has given your life to the Lord and want His will, you can commit your ways to Him and trust Him to direct you (Prov. 3:5-6). If you've made decisions in the past that you now regret, you can trust God to help you do what's right in your circumstances and to work through them for His glory and your good. Rest in this fact: "We know that in all things God works for the good of those who love him" (Rom. 8:28). You do not need to fear wrong decisions or being out of God's will.

Fear of What People Will Think

Prov. 29:25 says, "Fear of man will prove to be a snare, but whoever trusts in the LORD is kept safe." Don't live your life worrying about what people will think, or you won't be able to please God or yourself (Gal. 1:10). If other people are displeased with you or judgmental about the way you're handling your life, that's all right. It's not your responsibility to keep everyone happy. As long as you're not intentionally mean and hurtful, let go of the reaction of others. Those who have not been through anything similar to what you're going through may be way off the mark with their opinions. If they judge you harshly, that's their problem.

Abby is a born people-pleaser, and Kevin's family is very opinionated. Abby tries to please her mother-in-law and is devastated when she falls short. She dreads her mother-in-law's reaction to the news that Abby and Kevin are having marital problems, because she knows she'll be blamed for everything. Abby needs to accept the fact that she *can't* please her mother-in-law and focus on living her own life—with or without Kevin's family's approval.

If you please God, you've succeeded.

Fear Regarding Your Children

Your children are a very important part of your life, and you're not alone if fear regarding them sometimes seems overwhelming. You may fear them finding out about the problems, or you may fear the effects of your dysfunctional home on their choices as teenagers and adults. Even though these fears are realistic, they usually don't motivate change. I poured more energy into trying to force my husband to change than on doing what I could to take care of my children's needs. My priorities were out of order.

Many husbands use the children as a bargaining chip, saying, "You'll never see the kids again," "I'll prove that you're a bad mother," or "I'll fight you for the kids." The chances of that happening are almost nonexistent. Usually these are empty threats made to prevent change.

Sharon tolerated emotional and verbal abuse for 15 years because she feared losing her children to her husband. When he left her, she had no choice but to go through a difficult and long custody battle, believing the whole time that right would prevail. She did what she needed to do, even though she had to borrow the money to go to court, and was awarded primary custody. When her children visit their father every other weekend, she practices acceptance, since there's nothing she can do about it. She prays that God will be with them, and she stays alert to problems the best she can under the circumstances.

Fear of Regret

I know you agonize over every decision you make, trying to make sure you've considered every option in order to achieve the desired outcome. My husband used to tell me that I analyzed all angles of every situation before I could do anything. He was right. I was trying to control everyone and everything before anything happened.

There's also the powerful fear of not being able to live with the regret of not having done all you could to save your marriage. Faye, a woman married to an abusive alcoholic, expressed it this way: "I panic when I think I didn't love him enough or try hard enough. Our relationship is over. It feels as if it's my fault. I should have been able to fix it." That's a heavy burden to carry when your husband makes independent choices and is at least half of the relationship.

The fear of regret is often the result of perfectionism and unreasonable expectations like "I should have known better." Everyone makes mistakes. You can allow yourself grace. "Godly sorrow brings repentance that leads to salvation and leaves no regret" (2 Cor. 7:10). Do your best, and then trust God with your regrets.

Fear of the Unknown

What if _____? You fill in the blank. The future is unknown, and that's scary. It's impossible to control.

Alana constantly worried about what *might* happen. She became nervous every time she opened a letter, answered the phone, or didn't hear from Glen after work. She created all sorts of scenarios in her mind: he was dead, he was having an affair, they were losing the house, he wanted a divorce, and so on. Then she started making plans in her mind for how all these imagined events should be handled. It was difficult for her to keep her mind on the present or even enjoy her children. At times she was virtually unable to function.

None of us really knows what the next moment may bring, and we should always keep in mind that God's plans may be different than the plans we make (James 4:13-16).

If you're spending time focusing on solving problems you don't really have yet, you're letting what *might* happen rule your life. This can result in poor decision-making regarding what's on your plate *today*.

Fear of Staying the Same

You may be asking yourself, *What if my marriage never changes? Can I live like this forever?* This fear became a powerful motivator for me. I looked back at phases of my marriage: good times, OK times, bad times, and crisis times. At times I strongly considered divorce. One day I found myself thinking, *I should have left before we had kids. I should have left after my second child was born.* I projected into the future and saw myself thinking, *I should have done something then.* I realized this cycle of regret and inaction would repeat itself until I died of old age if I didn't make a change. It was then I decided to confront the problems head-on and draw firm boundaries. The fear of things staying the same was stronger than the fear of divorce. I was motivated to stand for right—even if it meant losing my marriage. Thankfully, my husband was able to change. But if he had refused to do it, I would have left, because the situation was not healthy for any of us.

If you're *afraid* things are always going to be the same, it might be time to initiate change yourself.

When Fear Is a Warning

Prov. 22:3 says, "A prudent man sees danger and takes refuge, but the simple keep going and suffer for it."

Some fears are reasonable, and you should heed them. For example, you *should* pay attention if you fear contracting a sexually transmitted disease if your husband is involved with other women. If he drinks and drives, you *should* be afraid to let your children ride with him. If there are illegal drugs in your home, you *should* fear your children finding them. You *should* fear your children being affected by the dysfunction in your home. It's reasonable for you to fear becoming ill due to stress or being injured by your husband if he's abusive.

These are the types of fears that should motivate you to initiate change.

Responding to Fear

Don't Give Way to Fear

Evaluate your fears and how they affect your decisions and reactions on a daily basis:
- What is the root of your fear?
- Is your fear realistic or unrealistic?

- Is it projecting far into the future, or are you actually dealing with it today?
- How does your fear affect your decisions and actions?
- Can you do anything about it right now?
- Are you willing to take necessary action?

Deal with fear by identifying it, feeling it, talking to God and others about it, analyzing how it's affecting your choices, and then say, "So what?" to your fear by doing the right thing anyway. It's the only way to keep it from paralyzing and imprisoning you.

Paul wrote to Timothy, "God did not give us a spirit of timidity, but a spirit of power, of love and of self-discipline" (2 Tim. 1:7). Self-discipline is translated as a "sound mind" in the King James Version. Paul was telling Timothy to respond to fear with God's strength. Having a sound mind gives you the ability to choose your response to fear. If it's something you're dealing with today, you need the courage to do what you must to remedy the situation. If there's nothing you can do, you can respond by trusting God.

Fear is the anticipation that something will happen. If and when it becomes reality, the fear ends, and you'll experience other emotions. Job said, "What I feared has come upon me; what I dreaded has happened to me. I have no peace, no quietness; I have no rest, but only turmoil" (Job 3:25-26). At the moment Job's fears became real, he no longer felt fear; he felt despair, hopelessness, and confusion.

Colette's worse fear was her husband getting in an accident and going to jail. She stayed up at night waiting on pins and needles for him to get home, especially when she knew he was drinking. When an accident finally happened, she was surprised by how well she handled it. However, it brought a new set of fears. "Will we lose the house?" "Will our friends turn their backs on us?" "Will he lose his job?" "Will he go to jail?" "Will he be angry if I refuse to drive him to work?" Colette decided to turn the new fears over to

God. She realized that this might be the thing that God used to get Gary to recognize his drinking problem. She determined to handle each problem with God's help as it came up.

Fear causes anxiety and worry. Remind yourself that it's just a feeling and not necessarily real. This will help you put it into proper perspective. 1 Pet. 3:6 says, "You are her [Sarah's] daughters if you do what is right and do not give way to fear."

Trust in the Lord

You trust God by an act of will, choosing to trust because you know God is good and trustworthy. God promises to give you strength (Phil. 4:13) and work all things for your good (Romans 8:28). That does not mean your way will be easy or that your marriage will be perfect, but that your future will be better if you do what's right instead of allowing fear to rule you. Prov. 3:5-6, cited earlier, says, "Trust in the LORD with all your heart and lean not on your own understanding; in all your ways acknowledge him, and he will make your paths straight."

Carol was extremely fearful when she made the decision to confront Jerry's sexual addiction and withdrawal from the family. She worried about how they would pay the bills, what Jerry's reaction would be, what their friends would say, and what would happen with his job. She struggled to feel God's peace even though she knew that she should take a stand and ask him to leave home until he got treatment and changed his behavior. She reached a point at which she decided to trust God, and she presented her husband with her conditions. He left. She explained, "The peace of God came flooding in when I did what was right. I don't know what the outcome will be, but I'm certain it will work out."

Ps. 16:8 says, "I have set the LORD always before me. Because he is at my right hand, I will not be shaken." If you can think about God's promises and provision—even in the face of fear—you will feel more trust. This will enable you to make wiser decisions because you will not be shaken.

Lifesaving Principle
Speak the Truth in Love

Then we will no longer be infants, tossed back and forth by the waves, and blown here and there by every wind of teaching and by the cunning and craftiness of men in their deceitful scheming. Instead, speaking the truth in love, we will in all things grow up into him who is the Head, that is, Christ.
—Eph. 4:14-15

*P*oor communication skills often underlie difficult relationships. Addictions and dysfunctions cloud communication with layers of expectations, resentments, and blame. Even if your husband is unable to communicate in a healthy way, you can learn to. Speaking the truth in love is a powerful principle that changes the dynamics of your relationship.

Know the Truth

Let Go of Denial

Jesus said truth produces freedom (John 8:32). Denial is a strong psychological tool that keeps you from facing unpleasant things. Addicts typically deny their addictions until they hit rock bottom.

Denial is different than lying. Lying is a deliberate deception for the purpose of covering up something one knows is wrong. Denial is a protective filter that keeps one from facing things he or she is unable to deal with. The downside is that it prevents one from using the truth to make wise decisions. As Prov. 22:3 says, "A prudent man sees danger and takes refuge, but the simple keep going and suffer for it."

Some church doctrines encourage denial. "Faith teaching" says we should speak the truth into being. This teaching would instruct you to *believe* your marriage is healed, your husband is whole, your problems are gone, and your bank account is full. It tells you that you can speak and believe into existence whatever you feel you need. God has not given you the power to cause things to happen with your words or with your faith. Don't live in fear that you're preventing healing because you haven't said the right words. It's OK to say you're hurting, sick, poor, or struggling in a difficult marriage. God honors truth. Prov. 12:22 says, "The LORD detests lying lips, but he delights in men who are truthful."

In order to reach a healthy level of acceptance about your difficult marriage, you'll have to travel through three other stages: denial, blame and anger, and sadness and grief. In order to move away from denial, admit the truth about your husband's problem, how it affects you, and how you react. That will bring you to facing and feeling your anger toward God, yourself, and your husband. Eventually you'll grieve the loss of all the things you want but don't have. During the period of sadness and grief, you'll mourn the loss of the dreams you held on to while you denied the truth. You may feel depression, hopelessness, and sadness. Once you work through the grief, you'll come to accept the facts about your life. With a new sense of peace, you can then make decisions with a new resolve.

Ruth married a pastor. After a year of marriage, she found him looking at pornography on the Internet. She believed his excuse that it was accidentally downloaded. A year later she discovered that he was regularly using pornography. First she blamed herself for not being sexy enough. Then she became angry with God. Why did He lead her to marry this man? God knew she wanted to marry a strong Christian. Then came anger with her husband, and she accused him of being a hypocrite. Next, sadness set in as she began to face the reality that her husband had a serious problem that had started when he was a teenager. She grieved the loss of her dream of a perfect marriage and accepted the fact that her husband had a sexual addiction that he would need help to overcome. She had to take care of herself and decide what boundaries she needed to set.

Let Go of Self-Doubt

Learn to trust your own feelings, thoughts, and perceptions. If you suspect an addiction, there probably *is* an addiction. If you feel put down, you *are* being put down. If you think you're being insulted, you likely *are* being insulted. If you feel your husband is being mean and demeaning, he is. If you think he's lying, he probably *is* lying. This will be particularly difficult if your husband is verbally abusive, manipulative, or controlling, as that continual assault on your sense of self-worth will make it harder to fight for your truth.

You may feel confused by what you see your husband doing and what he tells you. He says he isn't angry, but his behavior is hostile. He says he isn't drinking, but you see an empty bottle, and he smells like alcohol. He says he's going to end the affair but wants to stay friends with her. He says he'll change, but he does nothing to change. If what your husband promises he'll do and what he actually does are two different things, face the truth: his words are empty promises.

Knowing the truth means facing the facts. Your husband is an alcoholic, addict, abuser, gambler, or difficult person. You don't have enough money. You're angry, unhappy, and hurt. You live in fear. You're ashamed. You feel trapped. You wonder what God wants for you and from you. Whatever the truth is about your marriage, you have to trust your perceptions and feelings about it in order to move forward.

You'll feel anger. If you don't feel anger, you're keeping the peace at any cost. Anger *should* be felt when encountering wrong. Jesus got angry when people were disrespecting God's Temple by selling sacrifices in it, even throwing tables over (John 2:14-17).

On the other hand, if all you feel is anger, it's masking other emotions. Anger gives you energy and allows you to feel powerful and in control for a while. Underneath, though, you may be feeling fear, sadness, disappointment, or guilt. Try to feel all your emotions. It's important to understand the truth about what you're feeling in order to effectively communicate it.

Give yourself time to clarify your truth. When you feel confused, journal about it or talk to someone you trust. Eventually you'll begin to trust your feelings and perceptions and will come to see that many of your intuitions have been correct all along. As the truth about your problems becomes clear, you'll begin to be empowered to make changes in your own life and in the way you relate to your husband.

Speak the Truth

Be Willing to Confront

Jesus confronted people in a very direct way. He told the Samaritan woman in John 4 that she was living with a man who was not her husband. He treated her with dignity but directly confronted her sin. He told the woman caught in adultery to "Go, and sin no more" (John 8:11, KJV). He always spoke the truth (John 1:17).

There will be times you will have to tell your husband that what he's doing is wrong. Real love is willing to risk disapproval to stand up for what's right.

You've heard people say, "Be accepting, loving, and kind

like Jesus." They're inferring passivity and tolerance. In reality, Jesus was hard-hitting and cutting with His remarks, especially when someone was manipulating Him, tricking Him, or speaking against Him. He was quick to point out hypocrisy and lies. Consider these remarks to the Pharisees: "You brood of vipers, how can you who are evil say anything good? For out of the overflow of the heart the mouth speaks" (Matt. 12:34). "Woe to you, teachers of the law and Pharisees, you hypocrites!" (Matt. 23:29). "You snakes! You brood of vipers! How will you escape being condemned to hell?" (Matt. 23:33). And this comment to the Sadducees: "You are in error because you do not know the Scriptures or the power of God" (Matt. 22:29). And these to the disciples: "Are you still so dull?" (Matt. 15:16). "You of little faith, why are you talking among yourselves about having no bread? Do you still not understand?" (Matt. 16:8-9). "Could you men not keep watch with me for one hour?" (Matt. 26:40).

Paul also confronted the Church frequently about the things they were doing wrong: "I wrote you out of great distress and anguish of heart and with many tears, not to grieve you but to let you know the depth of my love for you" (2 Cor. 2:4). Paul says in 2 Cor. 7:8-11 that he does not regret the fact that the letter caused them sorrow, because that sorrow led them to repent. You need to be honest with your husband even when it's painful for him. Your loving honesty could bring about change.

Marge always made excuses to everyone about Shawn's temper, but his anger was increasing, and their teenagers resented him. Shawn didn't seem to be aware of the pain he was causing. Marge and the boys finally confronted him directly and told him they didn't like to be around him anymore and were afraid of him. Shawn was defensive at first, but after a while he listened.

Approach your husband in a loving way that lets him

know you're holding him accountable because you care about him and your marriage. Tough love says, "I love you enough to be willing to cause you discomfort or pain in the hope of helping you better your life and mine." Although you can't force him to agree with you or to change, you're responsible for confronting him with the truth. "Answer a fool according to his folly, or he will be wise in his own eyes" (Prov. 26:5).

Be Honest

Even though you may dread his rejection, threats of divorce, disapproval, and anger, your husband needs to know the truth about you and how you feel. You can't have intimacy without truth. Some women suffer in silence until they suddenly announce they want a divorce. Speaking the truth gives your husband the opportunity to change before it's too late.

This level of honesty is about you, not your husband. Consider the following statements:

- The focus is not on trying to force him to agree with you but on stating your feelings, thoughts, and needs.
- The focus is not on what he is doing but on how it's affecting you.
- The focus is not on who he is but on how you're affected by who he is.
- The focus is not on his failures but on your difficulty dealing with the effects of his failures.

This is different than confronting him when you want him to take a look at his own behavior. This is willingly sharing what's going on with you without blaming him. The following are some examples.

Instead of saying "You're an alcoholic, and you're failing your family, just like your dad did. Why can't you stop drinking and go to work?" you say, "I'm struggling with your drinking. It makes me uncomfortable, and I can't be around you when you're drinking. I'm starting to pull away from you, and I'm worried about our marriage. I don't know how much longer I can live with this."

Instead of saying, "Why can't you stand up to your father in my defense?" you say, "I feel as if you care more about your dad than me when you refuse to defend me."

Instead of saying, "You're such a jerk. Can't you see how you're hurting me? Can't you see how rudely you talk to me and how angry you are?" you say, "I'm uncomfortable with the way you talk to me. Your anger scares me, and I find myself afraid to talk to you."

The most important thing about speaking *your* truth is that you accept it as *your* own truth and not his. Don't attack him, blame him, or try to persuade him.

Renee can't stand the smell of alcohol or her husband's snoring after he's been drinking; both interfere with her sleep. In the past she kept quiet and lost sleep. She learned to simply state, "When you drink, I'm going to sleep in the other room. The smell and snoring keep me awake."

Sharing your feelings in this way is less likely to provoke arguments than direct accusations, but your husband may still minimize your feelings or tell you that you're wrong. Stand firm and state, "This is the way I feel, and it's what I need to do."

Be Direct

Gather your thoughts and then be succinct. Direct and straightforward communication is powerful. Don't expect your husband to guess what you mean or want.

I was in the habit of giving my husband long lectures with the goal of him finally getting it. My ultimate goal was to force a change, and by nature I am more of a talker than he is. Fewer words make your point more powerfully than a lecture.

Feel the power in the following statements compared to an emotional and argumentative lecture:

"I feel belittled when you ignore me."

"I felt humiliated by your comments in front of Judy."

"I'm repulsed by the smell of liquor on you."

"I'm angry about our financial problems."

"I'm concerned about our marriage. I want to get help."

Use clear statements that say what you mean. Don't use empty threats made in anger; if you don't follow through, your husband will know you're only venting and won't take you seriously. Say only what you really mean and what you're willing to follow through with. Rather than threatening divorce, say, "I'm finding myself thinking about life without you. That scares me, but I don't know how much longer I can hold on." If you've taken over his responsibilities, you can say, "I used to call your boss for you, but I was wrong. If you don't get up for work, you'll need to call yourself." That's better than saying, "The next time you get drunk and don't get up for work, I'm going to call your boss. and I hope you get fired."

Be Respectful

It's very likely that your tone of voice and body language have communicated contempt and disrespect for your husband, treating him like a bad boy who's ruining your life. If you tell him your truth in a mean and contemptuous way, you won't walk away feeling that you did the right thing.

Treat your husband like an adult who has choices, even if you don't approve of them. Use a tone of voice that communicates respect. He's more likely to receive what you have to say in a positive way if he doesn't feel as if you're attacking him.

Be Humble

Remember—your husband is as valuable to God as you are. Keep a proper perspective on who you are in relation to God and others.

Admit when you're wrong. Audrey said, "I was becoming as defensive as my husband. I feel better when I admit my faults, even if he's sarcastic and tells me it's about time I realize I'm not perfect."

Humility keeps your heart clean before God and provides a good example for your husband.

Be Persistent

Be persistent with speaking your truth. It won't bring about instant change, and it may even produce short-term new conflict in your marriage. You and your husband may be forced to deal with issues you've ignored. He may react with fear, insecurity, anger, or increased control tactics, and he may not know how to handle what you have to say. Acknowledge his feelings and reactions—then detach. Emily told her husband how his harsh comments hurt her. He laughed and told her she was too sensitive. She refused to react with anger but continued to tell him how she felt.

Up to this point you may have conditioned your husband not to take you seriously because of your empty threats and angry outbursts in the past. Change the way you communicate, and follow through with action. Nan told her husband she would leave the house for a few days if he threatened her again. He ignored her. The next time he threatened, he said mockingly, "Are you going to leave now?" He had heard. She left. If your actions change along with your words, you'll be communicating your truth effectively.

Be Willing to Listen

When you speak the truth, your husband may begin to communicate more honestly also. Some of what he has to say may be hard to hear. He may express his doubts about your marriage. He may say things about you that you don't like or that you disagree with. Suppress the desire to convince him that he's wrong. Don't react to your fear, even if he expresses doubts about your relationship.

Be willing to listen to him talk about his feelings, pain, and struggles. You may have some incorrect assumptions. Listening will give you a better understanding of who he is and what he struggles with. "He who answers before listening—that is his folly and his shame" (Prov. 18:13).

Be Silent

Even a fool is thought wise if he keeps silent, and discerning if he holds his tongue" (Prov. 17:28). There are times when it's wise to not say anything at all. "Do not answer a fool according to his folly, or you will be like him yourself" (Prov. 26:4). The secret is knowing when to speak and when to keep quiet. There will be times when you know your words will only provoke anger, an argument, or an irrational response. That's the time to remain silent.

Tom was in one of his moods. Chelsea wanted to talk to him about the unpaid bills and his coming in late the night before, but she knew she wouldn't get anywhere with him tonight. Knowing she needed him to be in a receptive mood, she let it go and decided to discuss it another time.

When you know your words will be destructive and cause anger, just be quiet. Don't try to talk to your husband if he's under the influence of drugs or alcohol, raging, or completely unreasonable. It's useless and can be dangerous. If you have a physically violent husband, use wisdom. Taking care of yourself comes before everything else.

Be Reasonable

Remember that even in the best marriages there are problems and irritations. Keep a proper perspective.

Even perfect husbands annoy their wives some of the time. Don't exaggerate idiosyncrasies that are just part of his personality. Try to overlook things that really aren't a big deal.

Anna used to nag Peter about everything he did that irritated her. They were always arguing, and she was always unhappy. Now she overlooks little things like his leaving the lid off the butter dish, throwing his clothes onto the floor, watching sports games, and telling his lame jokes. She still finds these behaviors annoying, but she's decided not to complain about every single thing every single time.

Ask yourself these questions: *How important is it? Is it life-threatening? Is it immoral? Is it something that affects me in the long term? Is it harmful to me or the children? What are the ramifications if I just let it go? How will it affect me to say something about it? Is it worth mentioning, or will it cause a bigger problem that will cause me to deal with even more problems? In a couple of days will I remember what it was that irritated me so much? What's my state of mind at the moment? Could it be that I'm tired and that things are appearing to be more serious than they are? Am I reacting to what's happening now, or am I angry about the past?* These are some of the questions you can ask yourself to help you figure out if what you're upset about is important enough to mention.

The balance to speaking the truth in love is learning that there are times that "love covers a multitude of sins" (1 Pet. 4:8) and "is not easily angered" (1 Cor. 13:5).

Don't sweat the small stuff.

Be Slow to Speak

"Everyone should be quick to listen, slow to speak and slow to become angry" (James 1:19). Prov. 15:28 says, "The heart of the righteous weighs its answers, but the mouth of the wicked gushes evil."

I still fight my tendency to react to my husband and children. I learned through many mistakes that it's better to stop and think. Try counting to 10 or even 100 before you speak. I learned to say, "Let me think about it and get back to you." That gave me time to think about my answer.

Be patient in presenting your truth. Your husband will probably be more receptive if he hears small portions that he can digest rather than years of your unexpressed truth dumped on him all at once.

Lifesaving Principle 8
Set Boundaries

God did not give us a spirit of timidity, but a spirit of power, of love and of self-discipline.
—2 Tim. 1:7

Jesus set boundaries in His interactions with others. He chose when to respond and how to respond, always in full control of himself and what He allowed others to do to Him. He willingly went to the Cross at the appointed time but withdrew himself from dangerous situations before that time. He held people responsible for their actions while consistently demonstrating authority and integrity (Mark 1:22; Luke 4:32).

Each person's boundaries are unique based on his or her history, personality, beliefs, tolerance, and the specific circumstances. As Rom. 14:5 says, "One man considers one day more sacred than another; another man considers every day alike. Each one should be fully convinced in his own mind."

Weak Boundaries

It takes a significant amount of strength, vigilance, and self-respect to maintain boundaries that are constantly assaulted and tested. Without boundaries, you have little control over your life. Prov. 25:28 says, "Like a city whose walls are broken down is a man who lacks self-control."

Setting boundaries in a difficult marriage is not an easy thing to do. Your husband may purposely challenge and undermine your right to set limits. Following through with consequences when your boundaries are violated will require strength and determination on your part. Paula says that before she takes a stand regarding her boundaries, she plans in her mind all the possible scenarios of what might happen as a result. She even considers how and where she would live if it results in divorce.

Do you struggle with setting boundaries in your marriage? If so, these may be some of the reasons:

- You don't trust your thoughts, feelings, and perceptions.
- You would rather give in to keep the peace.
- You were raised in a dysfunctional home.
- You are unsure of your boundaries.
- You think being a good Christian means passively tolerating anything.
- You're waiting for God to change your husband.
- You believe you should submit and give up your rights.
- You're afraid of his reaction or that he'll leave you.
- You know he won't respect your boundaries anyway.
- You're afraid to follow through with consequences.

Even though it will be difficult, setting boundaries is the most effective thing you can do to change your marriage. You don't need your husband to agree with your boundaries. Once your boundary is violated, you can examine your options and determine what you're willing or not willing to do in response.

Here are some examples of boundaries:

- Mandy's husband yelled at her when he was upset or drinking. Mandy learned to say, "I'm not going to talk with you when you're yelling at me. We'll talk later."
- Gina refuses to pay bills when Steve overlooks payment due dates.
- Jan refuses to make excuses when Jack misses work or family outings due to his drug abuse.

- Jenny asked Bob to move out of the house because he was having an affair.
- Connie refused to allow Ron to have pornographic materials in her home. If he could not comply, he would have to leave.
- Renee refused to let Tony use his bipolar disease as an excuse for becoming angry. She told him he had to get help to manage his moods.

You can't make your husband talk respectfully to you, quit drinking, end an affair, refrain from looking at pornography, stop being physically or verbally abusive, or do anything else you want him to. Your husband chooses how he will respond to your request. *You* choose your response to his.

Setting Boundaries

The following are examples of boundaries to consider:
- What you're willing to do
- What you're willing to accept and tolerate
- What you find offensive
- What you'll watch and listen to
- Where you'll go
- What type of treatment you consider respectful
- What is sin for you (the gray areas outside of God's direct commands)
- What you believe and value
- What your needs and priorities are

If you don't have boundaries, people are free to violate you however they choose. Strong boundaries are needed for many reasons:
- Your husband will know that his choices carry consequences.
- You won't enable sin.
- You and your children will be protected.
- You'll respect yourself, and others will respect you.
- You'll have self-control.

- You'll live true to your convictions.
- You'll be modeling boundaries for your children.

Answering the following questions will help you decide what boundaries you want to set:

- Does what you want to do encourage your husband to get help or to continue his destructive habits?
- What is best for the family—not just your husband or you?
- Where does your responsibility start and end?
- Where does his responsibility start and end?
- What is your motive?
- Are you ready to follow through with the stated consequences?
- How does this situation affect your values?
- How will your decision affect you? Your husband? Your children? Your marriage?
- How important is this particular issue?
- What does God think of this issue?
- What boundaries do you need for emotional, spiritual, or physical protection?

Keeping these general considerations in mind, read through the following common problem areas, and decide what boundaries you should consider setting.

Drug and Alcohol Addictions

Boundary-setting when addictions are involved is obviously difficult. Addicts are self-centered and immature. Putting their addiction first, they take risks that jeopardize their families. Solomon warned, "Do not gaze at wine when it is red, when it sparkles in the cup, when it goes down smoothly! In the end it bites like a snake and poisons like a viper" (Prov. 23:31-32). Proverbs 20:1 says, "Wine is a mocker and beer a brawler; whoever is led astray by them is not wise." When your husband's addiction renders him unable to make wise decisions for the family, you will have to decide:

- Will you allow drugs or alcohol in the house?
- Will you allow your children to be in your husband's presence when he's under the influence?
- Will you bail him out of jail if he's arrested?
- Will you interact with him when he's not sober?
- Will you or the children ride in the car with him at the wheel when he's under the influence of alcohol or drugs?
- Will you refuse to give him the car keys when he's drinking or using drugs?
- Will you buy alcohol or drugs for him?
- Will you drink or abuse drugs with him or go to parties and bars?
- Will you leave him behind and see yourself home when he gets too intoxicated in a social setting?
- Will you have sex with him when he's under the influence of alcohol or drugs?
- Will you call his boss and make excuses when he can't go to work?
- Will you make excuses to family and friends when he's unable to attend functions?
- Will you require him to get treatment? What and how much?

Rachel asked John to leave the home when he brought illegal drugs into the house. Cindy laid down some new boundaries with her alcoholic husband: she refused to allow her children to ride in the car with him and brought a second car to social engagements so she could leave if he drank too much. Sandy told her husband that she would no longer make excuses for him when he didn't come to family gatherings.

Sexual Addictions

There are unique boundary decisions to be made in the case of sexual addictions. Men are warned: "Do not lust in your heart after her beauty or let her captivate you with her eyes, for the prostitute reduces you to a loaf of bread, and the adulteress preys upon your very life. Can a man scoop fire into his lap without his clothes being burned?" (Prov. 6:25-27).

It's difficult to draw clear boundaries if your husband is telling you, "All men look at pornography." The truth is that *not* all men look at pornography and that it's very devastating to their wives when they do. Jesus said that even looking at women lustfully equaled adultery of the heart (Matt. 5:28).

Here are some things to consider in setting boundaries if your husband has sexual addictions:

- Will you consider a sexual addiction equivalent to an affair?
- Will you have sex with him while he's actively pursuing his addiction?
- Will you risk contracting sexually transmitted diseases?
- Will you look at pornography with him?
- Will you allow pornography in your home?
- Will you participate in sexual acts that are uncomfortable or demeaning to you?
- Will you settle for an insufficient sexual relationship if he withdraws sexually from you?
- Will you allow him to have a computer in the house if he uses it for chat rooms or pornography?
- Will you tell any family members about his problem? Who?
- Will you require him to get treatment? What and how much?
- How will you handle setbacks?

Adulterous Affairs

Adulterous affairs are different from sexual addictions, because sexual addictions are mostly about the sex, but affairs involve an emotional and sexual relationship with one person over a longer time period.

Knowing your husband is having sex with another woman is painful enough, but knowing he feels that he loves her or is choosing her over you causes even deeper emotional pain. Alicia says, "It hurts so bad. I can't stand to think of him with her. He told me he never really loved me, but I know he did. I know I should ask him to leave, but I keep hoping he'll change his mind."

Lucy, pregnant with her third child, felt devastated, but she asked Mike to leave. "I can't imagine how I'll make it alone. My heart is breaking, but I can't accept him living with me, knowing he leaves to go with her. He's going to have to make a choice."

"A man who commits adultery lacks judgment; whoever does so destroys himself" (Prov. 6:32). He also destroys his family. Ultimately you'll have to make the following decisions:

- Will you tolerate a close emotional relationship between your husband and another woman?
- Will you ask him to leave the house while he's having the affair?
- Will you tell your children? Family? Friends?
- What type of relationship will you have with him while he's involved in the affair? Will you continue to have sex with him?
- Will you require that he not see her again?
- How will you have him prove the affair is over?
- Will you require him to change jobs if he works with her?
- Are you willing to forgive him and work on healing your marriage if the affair is over?

Healing is possible if the affair is ended and both partners are able to understand why the affair happened, reestablish trust, and strengthen their marriage in the weak areas.

Sexual Relations

In a difficult marriage you may often struggle with sex.

If you continue to meet your husband's sexual demands even though you feel extremely angry and hurt by his behavior or his betrayal, you feel demeaned and used. These types of comments are common:

- "I cry during and after sex."
- "I feel as if I'm being raped."
- "I can't have sex with him after he's yelled at me and raged. I feel as if I'm still being abused."
- "I have to look away and think about something else during sex."
- "I feel like a prostitute."
- "When he put his arms around me, I had to resist the impulse to pull away."

Just as you can say no to any other request, you can say no to a sexual request. Sexual distance can be a positive thing if you need to detach and set boundaries. There are times when it's absolutely necessary to protect yourself from the risk of contracting a sexually transmitted disease. Acknowledging the emotional pain you're feeling with sex and holding him accountable is part of being truthful. Sexual relations should never be demeaning or demoralizing.

On the other hand, don't withhold sex just to punish your husband. Men will often use sex as a means of comfort, as a way to resolve conflict, and a vehicle to reestablish intimacy. Both of you may actually feel closer after having sex. It's important to attempt to meet each other's needs sexually in a healthy way that does not violate either partner's needs, if possible.

Here are some things to consider in setting boundaries in the bedroom:

- Are you withholding sex as a punishment?
- Have you been honest with him regarding your feelings about sex?
- Do you need to refuse to have sex in order to protect yourself emotionally or physically?
- Will withholding sex cause more damage to your relationship?

- Can you clearly articulate the reason you won't have sex with him?
- Are you willing to do without sex?
- Are you going to sleep in the same bed with him? Who will leave the bedroom?
- What are the conditions under which you'll resume sexual relations?
- Is continuing to have sex preventing him from bearing the consequences of his behavior?
- Are you willing to deal with his increased anger and threats if you withhold sex?
- Will this be something he won't accept?
- Will withholding sex shut down the only area of intimacy you have with your husband?

If you decide not to have sex for a time, your husband may say something like "How do you expect me to live without sex?" He may even threaten to have an affair. Terry answered that question with her sexually addicted husband: "I can't answer that for you—I only know that I can't do it right now. It's just too painful."

If you're willing to have sex later, always tell him what made you feel safe enough to resume physical intimacy. This will reinforce the changes you need in the relationship. When Terry knew her husband was no longer using pornography and was emotionally available to her, she was able to resume sex. She explained to him how this closeness helped her to feel loved.

Money Problems

Money problems are common in difficult marriages. Irresponsible spending habits, overspending on addictions, lost jobs, and refusal or inability to work all result in bills not being paid.

Christians often have very firm ideas about the man being the head of the household in financial matters. Many women are devastated as they watch their husbands wreck their finances and financial security with overspending, addictions, and irresponsibility. They're reluctant to intervene because of the belief that the man is the head of the house. They and their children pay a high price. "In the house of the wise are stores of choice food and oil, but a foolish man devours all he has" (Prov. 21:20). There's a time for a woman to store provision for her family.

The ideal solution would be to protect your own needs while allowing him to suffer for his irresponsibility. Kelly got a job and paid for her car and personal needs but not his car or the house payment. She decided those were his responsibilities, but she had to survive.

Gina bought food for the children and paid the rent and utility bills, but not his charge card.

Each circumstance is different and requires much discernment and wisdom. When you can't do any more you have to trust God to provide. Here are some questions to consider:

- Which one of you is better at managing money?
- Are you both employed?
- What needs are being neglected? Are they critical ones to any family member?
- What are all the reasons your finances are bad? Have you contributed to overspending?
- Is he not working because of his poor choices or for justifiable reasons?
- If you're working, will you give him all, part, or none of your paycheck?
- Will you go to work to pay bills he doesn't pay? Which ones?
- If you do go to work, will you be angry and resentful about it?
- Will you give him money to pay for his addictions?
- Will you co-sign on purchases you disagree with?
- Will you keep separate bank accounts?

- If he refuses to work, will you give him a charge card or spending money?
- Will you borrow money from relatives to cover debt?
- Will you keep yourself on a tight budget to cover for his irresponsibility?
- Will you give him control over the checkbook and all the responsibility to pay bills?
- What do you need to do to protect yourself financially?

Your problem may be that your husband is overly controlling and rigid with money. If he refuses to let you work or takes all your paycheck when you do, requires you to account for every penny you spend, or withholds money as punishment, you'll also have difficult decisions to make:

- Will you give him your paycheck?
- Will you let him control everything you spend?
- What will help you be less angry and resentful?

Overall, consider what changes you need in order to restore as much dignity and health to your financial situation as possible. You may need to start small. Janet started by refusing to give an account of small purchases and by keeping back spending money from her paycheck.

Physical Abuse

Although no form of physical abuse is acceptable, there are levels of seriousness. Some women who are physically injured by their husbands are afraid to leave, because their husbands threaten serious harm if they do. If you're in that situation, seek professional help immediately.

There are also women who continue to antagonize and provoke until their husbands react with pushing or grabbing. If you know you provoke your husband to this extent, stop it. He still needs to take responsibility for his lack of self-control by getting help.

If your husband threatens you with physical harm unless you comply with his wishes, you should consider that as a form of intimidation that equals actual physical abuse.

Think about the following:
- What do you do if it happens only once?
- What if it happens only when he drinks or uses drugs?
- What if he only threatens to hit you?
- Are you responsible in any way for his loss of control?
- Do you have a place to go if you need to get away from him?
- Will you file a police report and testify against him in court?
- Will you accept his apologies when he's remorseful after an incident?
- Will you clean up or replace things he breaks in the house?
- Will you lie about any marks he leaves on you or the house?
- Is he capable of seriously hurting you?
- Do you need a restraining order for protection?
- Will you argue with him when he's angry?

Michelle knew that when she pushed an issue with her husband, he would likely become angry and react by pushing her. She decided to walk away from him when he was getting angry, but she also told him that he had to get help in order for her to stay with him.

Toni covered up John's physical abuse for years. She decided to get a restraining order and file charges. She was no longer willing to live with his threats and abuse.

Verbal and Emotional Abuse

Verbal and emotional abuse are typically cyclical, reoccurring without warning. They can be very subtle and, consequently, very confusing. They're common in dysfunctional relationships. Here are some tactics the verbal and emotional abuser uses to gain control:
- Blame
- Withdrawal
- Threats

- Ridicule
- Contempt
- Accusations
- Discounting needs, feelings, and opinions
- Teasing
- Name-calling
- Ignoring
- Withholding information, approval, affection, money, or needs
- Denying the truth or lying
- Refusal to cooperate
- Hostile anger
- Demeaning looks and stares
- Speaking in a condescending tone
- Silent treatments
- Punishment
- Destroying objects

You'll probably need professional help to work through a verbally and emotionally abusive relationship. It's important for you to understand the subtle manipulation and control involved and how it affects you. "Stone is heavy and sand a burden, but provocation by a fool is heavier than both" (Prov. 27:3). You can't make your husband stop abusing you. In fact, when you stand up and say no, the attempts to control you will often intensify, because your willingness to say no produces a challenge. Practicing detachment may also intensify the abuse as the abuser sees your separation and ability to make your own decisions as a threat. It's also crucial for you to take care of yourself and value your needs in order to rebuild the damage to you as a result of the abuse. Finally, abusive men need professional therapy. Promises to change without therapy are usually empty.

Relationship Boundaries

Relationship boundaries are complicated as each relationship is unique. One thing is standard, though: unhealthy marriages have unhealthy boundaries. Setting boundaries is an important part of making your relationship healthier. The following are some additional general questions to consider regardless of the specific problem you're dealing with:

- Will you get help even if he doesn't go with you or approve of your going?
- Will you get help for your children if he disapproves?
- How much anger will you tolerate before you withdraw from a conflict?
- What type of conflict resolution will you use to resolve conflicts?
- What changes do you need to make in yourself?
- Will you go places you want to go without him?
- How many outside interests and friends do you want to have?
- How close do you want to be to his family and your family?
- How many chances will you give him?
- Will you require him to get help? What and how much?
- Under what circumstances would you separate or divorce?

Divorce and Separation

Separation or divorce should not be used to bluff, manipulate, or punish your husband, and you must be emotionally ready to endure the possibility of his refusing to make the changes you have requested and your marriage ending.

Sometimes separation can be a powerful attention-getting boundary if you're fully ready to use it. The purpose of a separation can be to physically or emotionally protect you and your children or to convince your husband that you'll not continue to live the same way. Separation can also be by mutual agreement for each of you to work on your own problems separately with the goal of reconciling your marriage.

Separation can be informal or legal. In a legal separation, the court grants temporary support and custody. It protects you from financial liabilities incurred by your husband. This can be helpful in cases where you need protection for yourself and the children, visitation limits for your children, or to legally require your husband to provide for financial needs. A legal separation may also be advantageous when you need to file a restraining order or you need a court to make your husband leave the home. Be careful about leaving your home, as many states initially allow the children to stay with the parent that stays in the home for them to have stability and as few changes as possible. It's wise to consult an attorney before you consider separation or divorce. In an informal separation, you and your husband agree how to handle finances and custody. This is most likely possible when you're working toward reconciliation.

If there's a chance that you'll reconcile, you should be clear as to the conditions you need changed. Writing a list helps. This gives your husband a clear goal to work toward. It also helps you to determine whether or not those criteria have been met so that you won't prematurely reunite only to discover that nothing has changed. Depending on the situation, some couples agree to date during their separation so they can work on establishing a changed and renewed relationship. In other cases, such as when there's been an affair, abuse, or addiction, you may need to ask your spouse to stop the offensive behavior and get treatment before you'll continue to work on the marriage.

Separation has some negative aspects. It's financially expensive, especially if both husband and wife have to pay for a place to live. It gives both partners freedom, which can be threatening in the sense that once some people live apart, it can be more difficult to come back together. It's emotionally challenging, as you have to let go of the outcome and face the possibility that your marriage will not be reconciled.

In Hosea, God likened the people of Israel to an adulterous spouse. He was angry with Israel for her unfaithfulness and worship of other gods. He condemned Israel, punished her, set boundaries for her behavior, and then in compassion took her back after she repented. God said, "Because of all their wickedness in Gilgal, I hated them there. Because of all their sinful deeds, I will drive them out of my house. I will no longer love them" (9:15). This separation ultimately resulted in reconciliation, the same way you hope a separation will result in a healing of your marriage.

If your husband refuses to seek help or make the requested changes, you have a decision to make. You can choose to give him more time or file for divorce. The latter is a difficult decision and should not be made in haste or to punish him. It should be made only when you have absolutely no other options and the situation is serious and impossible to live with. The actual filing for divorce causes some men to hit bottom when a temporary separation did not, as some need the actual papers in their hands before they recognize what they're losing.

The decision to leave your marriage can be more difficult than staying in it. Only you can make the final determination that your marriage is so damaging and toxic that you must end it to save yourself and your children.

So what do you do with the fear that if you set firm boundaries your husband will leave? If your boundaries are established so that you can live in a dignified, respectful, and healthy way and he refuses to respect them, then you're doing what you have to do. Once you know you can't live with certain behaviors and you spell it out for him and he refuses to try to change, you have no other choice.

If you do go through a divorce, it's not wrong to take a

stand and use the legal system to protect yourself and get a fair property settlement and child custody. God has instituted law and government. There's nothing wrong with using it to protect yourself.

Ways to Express Boundaries

Solomon wrote,

> There is a time for everything, and a season for every activity under heaven: a time to be born and a time to die, a time to plant and a time to uproot, a time to kill and a time to heal, a time to tear down and a time to build, a time to weep and a time to laugh, a time to mourn and a time to dance, a time to scatter stones and a time to gather them, a time to embrace and a time to refrain, a time to search and a time to give up, a time to keep and a time to throw away, a time to tear and a time to mend, a time to be silent and a time to speak, a time to love and a time to hate, a time for war and a time for peace (Eccles. 3:1-8).

In marriage relationships there may also be a time to tolerate and a time to set boundaries. The following are examples of boundary-setting statements:

- "I can't do that."
- "I can't accept that."
- "I won't talk with you when you're yelling at me."
- "I need to do this for me."
- "I don't want to be around you when you're like that."
- "I don't like the way you are treating me."
- "Don't call me names."
- "I won't do that anymore."
- "If you hit me, I'll call the police."
- "Stop doing that."
- "I can't live this way anymore."
- "That would be wrong for me."
- "No."

When you set new boundaries, expect your husband to put pressure on you to back down. He may not like your changes, especially if it means you aren't enabling him anymore. He may threaten to leave you. Usually this is an empty threat, but there are times when a man will be unable or unwilling to make the changes his wife asks him to make.

Your husband will also have boundaries. It may be hard for you to accept his limits. If he tells you he can't do something, believe him, and don't try to change him. He's telling you who he is and what he can do. You can choose what you will do with his answer.

Every marriage—difficult or healthy—is different. It will take time for you to work through all the questions you must ask yourself. When your boundaries are established, you won't question them; you'll know what you can and cannot tolerate.

Boundaries are not permanent walls; they change as you and your husband grow. Then you can say, "The boundary lines have fallen for me in pleasant places" (Ps. 16:6).

Lifesaving Principle 9
Make Your Children a Priority

We were gentle among you, like a mother caring for her little children. We loved you so much that we were delighted to share not only the gospel of God but our lives as well, because you had become so dear to us.
—1 Thess. 2:7-8

*Y*our children are affected by the problems in your home. They experience the tension, insecurity, and turmoil. They live with broken promises and plans that are changed at the last minute. Spontaneity, fun, and laughter are scarce, and their punishment is usually administered in anger or frustration. They may not trust you or your husband.

Parenting children in your dysfunctional circumstances will be difficult. If your husband's problems render him ineffective as a father, it's left to you to struggle with confusing dilemmas and tough decisions. While your children will be affected by these problems, you can minimize the effects by making your children a priority.

Listen to Them

Feelings often go unvalidated in a dysfunctional home, especially if those feelings reveal a truth the family is unwilling to face. Parents may mistake the expression of negative emotions for disobedience and disrespect. Fathers often get angry when children express negative emotions toward them. Jason tells his dad, "I hate it when you get drunk in front of my friends." Jason's dad isn't willing to admit he has a drinking problem. "Don't talk to me that way! Go to your room!" he yells, punishing Jason for expressing his feelings.

Because of denial or a desire to comfort, mothers sometimes react to their children's expressions of negative feelings by saying things like "Everything's OK," when mother and children both know it's not OK.

"You hear, O Lord, the desire of the afflicted; you encourage them, and you listen to their cry" (Ps. 10:17). You can help your children deal with their feelings by listening and reflecting your understanding and empathy. "It sounds as though you're really angry at your dad." "When I'm angry, I feel as if I want to hit something too." "That must hurt." "I feel afraid, too, sometimes." "I want to run and hide when I'm embarrassed." Talking about feelings makes them seem less frightening and more manageable.

If your child reports physical or sexual abuse, believe him or her. Children don't usually lie about these things, and if they do it's a sign they have significant emotional issues. Tanya was separated from her husband, who suffered from bipolar disease and alcohol addiction and was also verbally abusive. She contemplated whether or not she could let him come home. Her 15-year-old daughter came to her and expressed discomfort over being with her father. She said she felt as though her dad were looking at her body inappropriately. While Tanya did not believe her husband would molest their daughter, she did realize that Tanya felt uncomfortable, and she couldn't let him come back home.

Establish trust between you and your children. You don't have to tell your husband everything, especially if he's unreasonable and might use the information to hurt them. If you tell him things your children tell you, they may conclude that confiding in Mom is unsafe. "A gossip betrays a confidence, but a trustworthy [person] keeps a secret" (Prov. 11:13). You may feel that you're betraying your husband by keeping secrets, but it's not wrong to have private conversations with your children. Accept the fact that you may have to withhold things from him in order to put the well-being of your children first.

Halley told her mother, Jane, about an embarrassing incident that happened at school. Jane debated whether or not she should tell Jim but decided he should know about his daughter's life. He used the information to ridicule Halley for being too sensitive. Halley felt betrayed by her mom and went to bed vowing to never tell her mom anything again. Jane regretted telling Jim and realized too late that this was not the first time something like this had happened.

Wendy noticed that when she voiced criticism of her daughter to her husband, he harassed the child and picked on her. She decided to keep her criticisms to herself and instead praise her daughter to her husband.

Jill complained to her husband that the children didn't help enough around the house. That evening her husband angrily forced the children to do household chores, all the while yelling at them and telling them that they were selfish. Jill didn't like the way he dealt with them and felt guilty for complaining. She decided to handle the problem on her own next time.

Talk to Them

Do you wonder what you should tell your children about your marital problems? What do you say when they ask, "Why is Dad acting that way?" Your answer will vary according to the problem you're dealing with, the age of the child, and the degree of the child's awareness. Small children need simple answers; older children need more detailed explanations. Tell them whatever will help them cope with the problem. "Do not let any unwholesome talk come out of your mouths, but only what is helpful for building others up according to their needs, that it may benefit those who listen" (Eph. 4:29). Be as truthful as possible in a matter-of-fact way that does not tell your children details they don't need to know.

Affirm that there are problems:

"Yes, Mom and Dad do fight a lot."

"Your dad's angry this weekend."

"Sometimes our family doesn't get along well."

"Your dad and I have problems in our marriage."

"I'm upset and sad today."

"Dad sometimes drinks too much."

If you're not telling them the truth, you're denying the truth. There's an unspoken rule in dysfunctional homes that problems are not discussed. Mothers may lie to protect their husbands, themselves, or the children. Jackson asked his mom why his father was sleeping on the front lawn. Instead of telling him he was passed out from drinking too much, she said he was camping. For whatever reason, she felt she could not tell Jackson the truth. Jackson already knew something wasn't right or he wouldn't be asking about it. Confusing children by telling them lies causes them to distrust their feelings and perceptions.

The unknown is always scarier than the known. Children's reasoning abilities are not yet matured. Truthful answers about whatever problems you're dealing with can minimize their fears.

Assure your children that other families have problems they must deal with too. This is where a support group or counseling can be very helpful. Children recognize that their feelings are valid and that their problems are not unique. Assure them that they're not to blame for the problems in their home.

Your husband may be angry with you when you start being truthful with your children. You may feel as though you're being disloyal and undermining him as your husband, but if you tell your children nothing, they'll feel abandoned by you. Wendy's husband was an alcoholic. Even though he drank in front of their children, he didn't want her to tell them he had a drinking problem. Wendy's nine-year-old son, Brian, was beginning to ask questions about the fighting and drinking. Wendy told Brian that his dad had a drinking problem that was difficult for him to control and that she hoped Dad would realize his need for help someday. Her husband was angry that she told Brian he was an alcoholic, but Wendy's son felt better, because he was able to talk to her openly about his feelings and the things that were going on in their home. Wendy also decided to take her son to a support group for children of alcoholics. Wendy knew she did the right thing and told her husband that she would not lie for him and was going to get help for the family whether he got help for himself or not.

Realistically share with your children the hope for a better future. My mom kept saying, "God will work it out—everything will be OK," when I brought up the problems in my family of origin. There was no one to validate the pain I felt or what I saw happening in my family. God did not make it better, and when I was a teenager I became disillusioned with God.

Instead of making this mistake, acknowledge the truth about the problems, admit that it will be hard for all of you at times, but share the hope that you're going to take steps to deal differently with the situation.

Children in dysfunctional homes experience more than their share of broken promises. It's common for their parents to promise things they don't deliver. Sharon told her son for the ninth time that season, "Your dad isn't coming to the game after all." She watched the tears spill down his face.

"I don't care anyway. I don't even want him here," Billy said.

Sharon put her arms around her son and said, "I'm disappointed too. It hurts."

Billy cried even harder, then wiped his tears and ran out to the field. Sharon's honesty and empathy validated Billy's feelings, even though she couldn't erase the hurt his dad caused.

Be as honest as you can, and let your child express the pain; then acknowledge the hurt. Covering up and making excuses or acting as if it isn't a big deal minimizes the child's feelings and further increases the damage.

Children in dysfunctional homes have a lot of fears: the dark, bugs, monsters, bad people, parents dying, being hurt by a parent or stranger, and being left alone. Talk about their fears, and pray with them. Do what it takes to minimize them, even if it means leaving a light on, checking closets, or whatever else helps them to know the fear is not real. Share how you handle fear too. Professional help is needed if the fears interfere with your child's ability to function.

Discipline Them

Your children need consistent discipline. Firm boundaries augment their sense of security, and it is important to hold them accountable for their actions. Prov. 23:13-14 says, "Do not withhold discipline from a child; if you punish him with the rod, he will not die. Punish him with the rod and save his soul from death." If you have trouble disciplining your children or are unsure how to deal with them at different ages, get help in this area.

Your husband may disagree with you on discipline styles. Men tend to be more authoritarian and concerned with teaching children to be responsible and resilient. Women tend to give in, understand, and lend emotional support. Children need both. Your husband's and your individual personalities coupled with the way you were both raised will also affect your relationships with your children and your discipline styles.

In a healthy marital relationship these differences in

styles and opinions could be talked about openly with an attitude of compromise and cooperation. However, in a difficult marriage with minimal cooperation and poor communication, differences are more difficult to resolve. Your situation may require you to adjust your expectations.

In stating your concerns with your husband's discipline style, keep it short, and specify it as an opinion or concern rather than saying that your husband is wrong. For example, you could say, "I feel that you were too hard on Tommy. Staying in his room all night is too much for a boy his age, " or "I feel that restricting Gina for two weeks is too long. One week would be more appropriate, and here are my reasons."

My husband felt strongly that he was the head of the household where discipline was concerned. I wanted to submit to him, but it wasn't that simple. There were many things he did that I felt were wrong. My daughters complained that he was unfair and difficult to deal with. I pointed out my concerns to him, but he didn't see it my way. He felt that my comments were undermining his position as head of our home and that I was judging him. The more I jumped in, the more inadequate he felt, and the angrier he became.

Several options are available to you when you disagree with the way your husband disciplines. Each option has varying levels of consequence for your relationship.

- Overlook it and say nothing.
- Tell him you disagree, but enforce his discipline.
- Tell him you disagree and will not enforce his discipline.
- Tell him you refuse to allow him to follow through with his discipline.

Assess the severity of the situation, and decide which reaction is appropriate. If any of them will cause your husband to mistreat your children more, don't do it, but if that's the case, it's a sign that he's mistreating your children, and you must protect them at all costs.

I supported some things I did not agree with, refused to support others, and made some decisions that contradicted his stand. He was angry with me many times because of disagreements regarding discipline, and it caused substantial problems in our relationship. I was deeply bothered by his interactions with the girls and was resentful toward him.

My daughters also resented me for enforcing their father's discipline. For example, if he put them on restriction, they would come to me and ask for an exception. Instead of saying, "Go ask your dad," I would say no to the request, feel bad, and be angry with him for applying a restriction I felt was unfair. I should have allowed him to enforce his discipline when I disagreed with it (as long as it was not abuse). Too often I was the one who figured out how to administer it and even followed through when he forgot about it!

Debbie's husband was often unfair in disciplining their children. In one instance he told their son that he had to pay back money for a figurine his younger sister broke and instructed Debbie to withhold his allowance. Debbie disagreed and told her husband that she would not enforce it. Her husband had to collect the money.

Karen's husband told their daughter she could not go to a get-together because she left her clothes on the floor. Knowing that he was resentful toward his daughter over an old issue and that his pattern was to take away something important over a minor incident, Karen told her husband that she would not make her daughter stay home that night. Karen drove her to the event. Had she not intervened, her daughter would have been unfairly treated. Teenagers often become rebellious over problems in the home and unreasonable discipline.

Gaye's husband took away their teenage daughter's car

for one month because she made a rude remark. Since Gaye was the one who would have to take the girl to and from school, she refused to agree to the discipline. The consequences of his discipline were going to fall on Gaye, and it was going to be a major inconvenience. She asked him to apply a different discipline.

Bret usually yelled at the kids when they didn't obey him or follow through with a task. Lisa hated to hear him dealing with the children in anger but realized that they did not follow through with what their dad asked them to do. Even though she did not agree with the way Bret was disciplining them, she did not intervene. She enforced his consequence of no television that night. Children often disobey and have bad attitudes. They make choices and need to experience consequences. If your children know that their dad is harsh and hard to deal with, they should try to obey his requests. Allow your husband to make mistakes in disciplining as long as he's not abusive. Chances are that you make mistakes in your interactions with your children too. Because your marriage is difficult, you may be overmonitoring and overly critical of your husband's discipline style.

"Like one who seizes a dog by the ears is a passer-by who meddles in a quarrel not his own" (Prov. 26:17). I frequently jumped in like a referee and tried to resolve arguments between my children and my husband without really knowing the whole story. "He who answers before listening—that is his folly and his shame" (Prov. 18:13). Even if my concern was legitimate, I often expressed it the wrong way. I undermined my husband's authority and made it more difficult for him to resolve the problem with the child, because she picked up on my criticism of him, and that fortified her belief that she was right and he was wrong. I also prevented the two of them from learning how to deal with each other. They needed to have a relationship—even if it wasn't perfect—and had the right to work it out without my intervention. When I stopped getting in the middle, they began to learn to resolve their problems, even if the resolution was not what I would have preferred. This was not an easy pattern to change. There were times I had to leave the room or even the house because it was too hard for me to listen to their arguments without interfering.

Even if their father is difficult and unreasonable, children should learn to respect his position as head of the home unless he asks them to do something immoral. Eph. 6:1-3 says, "Children, obey your parents in the Lord, for this is right. 'Honor your father and mother'—which is the first commandment with a promise—'that it may go well with you and that you may enjoy long life on the earth.'" There are times you'll say to your child, "He's your dad. He's doing what he thinks is right. Obey him." Children don't like being disciplined. There will be rebellion, disagreement, and anger at times; remember that these feelings don't prove that his discipline is wrong.

Your children—just like children born to healthy marriages—need to learn to obey authority and deal with difficult people. This life skill will benefit them their entire lives as they deal with teachers, employers, and government. If their father is unreasonable, they'll need to use self-control and learn that saying the wrong thing or having a wrong attitude can cause problems.

It's only in extreme situations that you should forbid your husband from disciplining your children, that is, in cases of abuse or when it would cause considerable harm. In these cases, you may need to insist on getting outside help through family counseling. Taking a strong stand against your husband's discipline could cause additional problems in your marriage or cause him to mistreat your children more. Be aware of those consequences, but always remember that protecting your children from serious emotional and physical harm is a higher priority.

Don't Abuse Them

"Fathers, do not exasperate your children; instead, bring them up in the training and instruction of the Lord" (Eph. 6:4). "Exasperate" means to irritate, frustrate, and annoy. Abuse does that and more.

Sexual abuse includes inappropriate comments, touching, inferences, or sexually graphic materials. Physical abuse includes slapping, punching, kicking, pulling hair, shoving, beating, and any other unusual methods of inflicting physical pain.

Emotional and verbal abuse include the following: name-calling, inappropriate teasing or ridicule, manipulation, total lack of concern for the child's needs or feelings, passive-aggressive anger, habitual yelling, purposeful withholding of approval or cooperation, purposely inducing guilt and feelings of responsibility for others, throwing things, breaking the child's possessions, constant criticism, abusive body language, purposely forgetting, denial of events, and mind games. The intent of verbal and emotional abuse is to punish, confuse, and control. Name-calling can be using swearwords or negative names such as "stupid," "idiot," "fatty," or "dummy." Teasing may appear to be joking but is cutting and mean.

Cara stood by for years as her husband ridiculed and played mind games to punish their daughter. At night Megan would cry, asking, "Why does Daddy hate me? I can't make him happy. What's wrong with me, Mommy?" Going to a counselor helped Cara draw boundaries to protect Megan. She told her husband he had to get help or leave the home.

I yelled too much at my children, especially when I felt frustrated by marital problems. I had grown up with yelling, so it was a natural reaction for me to yell when I was stressed. Still, there's no excuse for it. I hurt my daughters and have suffered many regrets. I should have done whatever it took to change my situation to be a better mom. My husband dealt with our daughters with the same passive-aggressive anger that he had experienced as a child. My children struggled with him emotionally and argued with him, but I did not intervene by requiring we get help. I was wrong.

Breaking a child's personal possessions is abuse, because it communicates a lack of respect for the child and a desire to hurt or physically harm. Donna asked her husband to leave the home after he broke several of her son's possessions over a minor discipline disagreement. The teenager threatened to run away if his dad stayed. Realizing that her husband's anger problem had crossed the line and that he needed help, she asked him to leave the home until he received treatment for his anger.

Failing to respect a child's need for privacy (like walking into the room when the child is dressing) is also abusive, as it violates personal rights.

"Anger is cruel and fury overwhelming" (Prov. 27:4). Anger is also abusive because it shows constant disapproval rather than love and acceptance, whether it's expressed through body language, passive acts, or outwardly aggressive acts. When their parents are mad at them, children assume it's because they've been bad. There's no way a child can reason by thinking, *My dad has a drinking problem, and that's why he's angry. It's not my fault. Mommy is angry with me today because she and daddy argued last night.* Instead, the child thinks, *I must be bad, because they're always mad at me.*

Passive-aggressive anger is destructive and confusing because the child sees behavior that he or she feels is hostile, but that feeling is not validated. Billy's dad was angry because Billy did not clean up after the dog, so his dad left the gate open and let the dog run away. When Billy asked him why he did it, he said, "I wanted the dog to be able to play." Billy felt confused and angry but could not discuss it with his dad, because his dad would not be honest about his motives.

If you notice yourself or your husband disciplining your children in abusive ways, get help. If it happens when you're upset at your husband, then it's a warning sign to you that you need to do whatever it takes to cope differently with your problems so that you don't harm your children.

Don't Depend on Your Children to Meet Your Needs

"Children should not have to save up for their parents, but parents for their children" (2 Cor. 12:14). You must learn to take care of yourself. Don't try to make your child your comforter, even if you have a child who tries to comfort you. This sets up a dysfunctional relationship. Don't make a child choose between you and your husband. Try not to discuss your marriage problems or your personal conflicts with your children unless you're simply validating their feelings. Try not to discuss your problems with their father in front of them. Be very careful not to allow them to change their lives in response to worrying about you. Lynn's son came to her and said, "Mommy, you're sad. I'll stay home and take care of you instead of going to Josh's house to play."

Lynn said, "You're so sweet to care about Mommy. I *am* sad, but I'll be OK. I want you to go play."

Don't put the responsibility for taking care of your husband and his problems on your child. Annette and her brother, Greg, felt that it was their responsibility to keep their dad in a good mood when he drank so he wouldn't get angry with their mom. They sat with him for hours, hating it. I remember intervening in fights between my parents when I was four years old in hopes of keeping the arguments from getting worse. My mother said she felt safe and less alone. These are inappropriate roles for children.

These are examples of mothers depending on their children to take care of them and their husbands when they should be taking care of their children.

Getting healthy must be a top priority for you. You have to be willing to fix yourself, or you won't be able to help your children. Leslie feels guilty leaving her children to go to a support group, but she knows she needs the meetings to help her deal with all the problems in her home. She's a better mom now. When her husband is in a bad mood, she takes the children to a sitter, where she knows they'll be safe while she's gone.

Show Them How to Cope

"In everything set them an example by doing what is good" (Titus 2:7). Your children learn from your example. Are your children seeing things in your dysfunctional home that you don't want them to see? Jean worried about her son imitating her husband's behavior when she saw the two-year-old kick the vacuum after her husband had kicked it in anger. What are your children learning from watching you?

Your attitude toward your husband will influence your children's view of their father. If you regularly criticize him and put him down, your children will also feel critical toward him. If you argue with him or respond sarcastically, they'll also argue. If you're honest about his problems but treat him with compassion and still stand up for yourself when you need to, they'll learn healthy boundaries and self-respect.

Your children tend to react to problems the way you do. Can you be happy and go on with your life when your husband is upset? If you can, they'll be able to do that too. Are you angry and upset all the time? They'll be that way too. Do you lie and cover up? They'll lie and cover up too. Are you depressed and hopeless? They'll feel hope when you do. Are you trusting God, or do you fret and worry? If you can't trust Him, how can they? Are you willing to be treated with disrespect? Then your children won't respect you or know how to stand up to mistreatment.

Be honest about your situation. "I know your dad is hard to deal with, and I sometimes feel so angry at him that I feel as if I hate him too. But then I remember that it's really hard for him to deal with his problems. I know he wants to do better, but he makes lots of mistakes. That's why he goes to those meetings at night." By being honest about the problem, you also have an opportunity to talk with them about the ways they can deal with it. Your goal is to help your children handle their fear, anger, and confusion by validating their feelings and providing them with coping strategies. Your motive should not be to turn them against their father, to get support for yourself, or to punish your husband. Always keep your children's best interest in mind.

Kay's teenage daughters were upset that she tolerated disrespect from her husband. They disrespected him for doing it and her for allowing it. They asked her to show them that women don't have to accept mistreatment in marriage. Kay realized that she was hurting her daughters and knew she was at a crossroads. She confronted her husband about his emotional and verbal abuse and told him if he didn't stop doing it, she would ask for a separation. Her daughters were encouraged by her new boundaries. It's never too late to model healthy relationship skills.

The sins of the parents are passed on to the third and fourth generations (Exod. 20:5) as children repeat the relationship behaviors they've observed. Maybe you come from a dysfunctional family and are repeating the mistakes of your parents as they repeated the mistakes of their parents. The healthy behavior you start teaching your children today will help to counter this generational repetition.

Provide Stability for Them

Because your home is dysfunctional, there's no predictable pattern to your lives, and your children don't know what to expect from day to day. You can help remedy that by following through with promises. Don't drop plans with your children because your husband doesn't show up, picks a fight, or changes his mind. Have a Plan B so that if Dad blows it, you and your children can still go. Try to give your children as much normalcy as possible. Jackie asked her father and brother if they would take her son to events his dad missed. Missing events is a big deal to children. Try to keep these disappointments to a minimum.

Don't let the tension of your difficult marriage spill over onto your children. Shirley became aware that she and her husband picked on their oldest son at the dinner table when they were at odds with each other. She decided that she would change the direction of the conversation when she saw that happening. When she knew things were really uptight, she arranged for her son to eat alone.

Make sure your children spend time with other people who will have a positive influence on them: church members, family, and friends. They'll come to see that other people deal differently with their problems. They'll also realize that you're respected and cared for by others, and it will deepen their respect for you.

Tend to Their Needs

"The eyes of the Lord are on the righteous and his ears are attentive to their prayer" (1 Pet. 3:12). Your focus on your husband and your difficult marriage may prevent you from giving your children your complete attention. You may be impatient and irritable with them because you have nothing left to give or you're so obsessed with your husband that you're unable to keep your mind on them.

Betty was so obsessed with her husband that she missed

out on being a mom to her children. Betty says that when she looks at their childhood pictures, she feels she wasn't even there, and she grieves over what she missed. She realizes now that she was emotionally unavailable to her children. After a short time in a support group, Jenny expressed to me that she focused her mind on what her five-year-old son was saying and actually got down on her knees to look in his eyes when he spoke. She realized this was an unusual level of attention on her part, and she was shocked to think she was previously so unavailable to her son.

Rita remembers rocking her babies and thinking, *I have to hurry so I can be with my husband.* Force yourself to be there with your children in mind, body, and emotions. You won't regret it. They need you today, and you'll enjoy being with them.

Have fun with your children today. Don't wait for your husband to join you. Belinda regrets not doing more things with her children. She was too often angry, impatient, and focused on the most recent crisis with her husband.

Respond to each child's individual needs. If a child is having trouble in school, go to parent conferences, increase your help with homework, or get a tutor. If a child has medical problems, take care of them. Develop each child's unique talents and personality. Discipline and train each child to maximize his or her strengths and improve in weak areas. Accept each child for who he or she is and have reasonable expectations.

If you notice that your child is seriously depressed, acting up consistently, displaying psychological problems, using drugs or alcohol, unable to function at home or school, or threatening physical harm to others or suicide, you must get appropriate help immediately. Children act up in negative ways as a means of dealing with problems in their homes. Get help even if your husband does not admit or agree a problem exists. Follow your intuition, and follow through with what's right for your child.

Protect Them

I used to believe that submitting to your husband meant putting him before your children—even if he mistreated them. I feel differently today. Don't submit to anything that's wrong. Hold your husband accountable, point out wrong behavior, and protect your children. God does not condone hurting children. Jesus said, "Things that cause people to sin are bound to come, but woe to that person through whom they come. It would be better for him to be thrown into the sea with a millstone tied around his neck than for him to cause one of these little ones to sin" (Luke 17:1-2). God's Word tells us to "defend the cause of the weak and fatherless; maintain the rights of the poor and oppressed. Rescue the weak and needy; deliver them from the hand of the wicked" (Ps. 82:3-4). Stand up for right, and obey God rather than man. Seek the good of others before that of yourself (1 Cor. 10:24). Sometimes that means you'll suffer consequences in order to protect your children. If you're unwilling to suffer negative repercussions like the loss of comfort, your husband's approval, or even your marriage, you're putting your needs above your children's. Children resent passive mothers who refuse to protect them.

When the problem is serious, you must speak the truth to your husband about what you see and set your boundaries. It's never helpful to yell, nag, plead, explain, or get angry. You can get counseling yourself, put your children in counseling or in a support group, ask your husband to go to counseling, or separate until he's ready to get help. Don't back down because he tells you that you're wrong. You must be willing to hold to your truth. If you're unsure, get outside advice to confirm your suspicions. Many children have been abused by one parent and then betrayed by the fact that the other parent saw it and did nothing to prevent it. This is devastating to children, because there's no one they can trust to take care of them.

If your husband is sexually or physically abusive, he can seriously hurt your children. Get him out of the home. If that's impossible, remove yourself and the children.

1 Kings 3:16-27 describes Solomon's dilemma. Two women came to him arguing over a baby they both claimed as their own. Solomon decided to determine which woman was truly the mother by proposing the baby be cut in two. The real mother said no; she would rather suffer the loss of her baby than see him hurt. Solomon gave the baby to her. Real mothers are willing to suffer loss to save their children.

Apologize to Them

There's nothing you can do to change the past, and you can't undo the mistakes you've made. There's no magic wand you can wave to take away your children's pain. When dealing with past events that affected your children negatively, acknowledge your mistakes, ask their forgiveness, and honestly answer their questions. Healing comes when you're honest about your sins (James 5:16). You can explain why you did what you did, especially with older children.

When you apologize to a grown child and he or she chooses not to forgive, give him or her room to work out those feelings, even though it's uncomfortable for you. It can take time to reestablish trust. Continue to let your child know that you want to restore the relationship, and offer unconditional love.

Most important, don't let regret and guilt over past mistakes keep you stuck. You can only choose to do what's right for your children and yourself today.

Lifesaving Principle

Enter God's Rest

Come to me, all you who are weary and burdened, and I will
give you rest. Take my yoke upon you and learn from me,
for I am gentle and humble in heart, and you will find rest for
your souls. For my yoke is easy and my burden is light.
—Matt. 11:28-30

The principles you've read about are easy to understand but not always so easy to put into practice. After learning the previous nine principles and beginning to apply them to your life, you can then turn your life and marriage over to God and enter His rest.

God loves your husband more than you do, and He wants your marriage to be a source of joy and contentment to you and your husband. You'll never be perfect, but even failures are not wasted if you learn from them.

Make Restitution

As much as possible, you should attempt to repair any damage you may have done. Old Testament Law requires restitution for certain acts such as stealing or negligence (Exod. 21-22). You're responsible for the ways you've hurt others—including your husband.

There are several ways restitution can be made: apologizing, repaying debts, doing nice things, or changing yourself and making better choices today. It's not possible to go back and alter the past. But when you change the way you treat people today, it shows an awareness that you were wrong in the past and that you're sincere in wanting to change.

Regardless of what your husband did to you in the past—and maybe continues to do now—you can admit to him your part in your marriage problems unless it would result in harm to you or someone else.

Emily knew that regardless of Paul's problems with alcohol and bipolar disease, her reactions had hurt him, partially out of her frustration and hurt but also out of her own pain from her father's rejection when she was a child. She apologized to Paul for her part in their marriage problems and began to work on changing her reactions. Paul chose to stay resentful toward her, but Emily continued to treat him differently anyway.

Whether or not someone forgives you has nothing to do with the way you conduct yourself. Prov. 14:9 says, "Fools mock at making amends for sin, but goodwill is found among the upright."

Risk a New Beginning

Change can be frightening, but it's good. In the previous chapters you learned a new way of relating to your husband. You faced the truth about yourself and your marriage and confronted your fears. You took risks by setting new boundaries and allowing your husband to face the consequences of his actions, even though you were uncertain of the outcome. You have a new strength, a new dependence on the Lord, a new perspective, and new hope for a good future.

If you came to the realization that you can't live with certain behaviors of your husband's, you may have to be willing to lose a bad marriage in order to gain a good one. You don't know how he'll respond, but it's his choice to decide whether or not he'll do what you ask. Your husband may be one of those difficult people who must hit bottom before he becomes willing to change. Watching that happen may be one of the most difficult things you'll ever do. He may even agree initially to make changes and then later change his mind. The road to repentance can be a long, curvy one. Let God work in his life, and take one day at a time.

Vicky knew she was no longer willing to live with Frank's anger and verbal abuse. She gave him a list of the specific changes she needed and asked him to decide if he was willing to make the changes. If he wasn't, he had to leave. If he was willing to change, it was up to him to get the help he needed. Even though Vicky didn't want her marriage to be over, Frank reacted in anger and left. Several months later, he told Vicky he didn't want to lose her and would go to counseling. Vicky was hopeful but told Frank she would no longer tolerate the abuse and was willing to separate if it reoccurred.

Surrender to Reality

When you reach the point at which you truly surrender your hopes and desires to God, you can enter His rest. This may mean accepting that your marriage and your life are not what you want and may never be. You're then free to decide what you'll do with the possibilities you have.

Beth says, "I'm accepting my husband more—including his limitations. I know he'll struggle with his sexual addiction. He is who he is. I don't like it, but I've decided I still want him in my life. I know that we both have a lot of work to do to make our marriage better." Even with her acceptance, Beth has boundaries. "I won't live with him using pornography. He'll have to stay pure. I'm willing to support him during this struggle, but I won't tolerate the sin. That wouldn't be good for me. I still worry at times that he's looking at pornography again, but I know I have to let go of the fear, even though it's hard. I have made the decision to try to restore my marriage, so I have to trust God with the final outcome."

Once you accept the reality of your life and your marriage, you're free to make choices. When you know you can choose to stay or leave, you can approach the relationship in a new way. You don't feel trapped. You accept your situation, learn to take care of yourself in it, take responsibility for your choices, and give your husband the dignity and freedom to make his choices. Accept the fact that God is with you at this point in your life. You can rest in Him, give it to Him, and trust Him to use it for your good and His glory.

What should have been an eight-day journey from Egypt into the Promised Land became a 40-year journey to teach the Israelites to completely rely on God by surrendering their wills. They made several repeated errors. When things got tough, they murmured, complained, and took their eyes off God. They stopped believing He would take care of them. Instead, they wished they were back in Egypt. They doubted God's provision even though they had seen Him perform miracles to save them time and time again. We, too, forget God's provision: His salvation, His word, His promise of eternal life, and His promise to be with us, comfort us, lead us, and strengthen us.

Phil. 4:6-7 says, "Do not be anxious about anything, but in everything, by prayer and petition, *with thanksgiving,* present your requests to God. And the peace of God, which transcends all understanding, will guard your hearts and your minds in Christ Jesus" (emphasis added). Giving God thanks for everything releases the peace that Jesus promised you in your trials. It does not mean you're thankful for the specific problem but for the *good* that will come out of it.

Candace faced many obstacles: financial difficulties, an estranged relationship with her father, and an alcoholic husband who had lost his job, been involved in an accident, and was currently in a treatment center. When she focused on the obstacles, she felt overwhelmed. Focusing on the positive things such as her health, her daughter, her mother's help, a church support group, and her husband's willingness to get treatment, she was able to change her perspective. She rejoiced that God was using these circumstances to force her husband to face his problem.

Live for Today

It's easier to enter God's rest if you're living one day at a time. Remember—you've made it through every day so far. Make it through that one 24-hour chunk of time by relying on God's strength. Don't add the weight of the past or the future to today.

In the Sermon on the Mount, Jesus told us not to worry about material things and the future. He said, "Do not worry about tomorrow, for tomorrow will worry about itself. Each day has enough trouble of its own" (Matt. 6:34). You don't know what the future will bring. You're living life one moment at a time anyway, so focus on living each moment to the best of your ability.

Let Your Husband Take Care of Himself

What if your marriage doesn't work? What if your husband doesn't change, or he changes for a while and then regresses? Things may or may not change the way you hope they will, but you can't allow the fear of the unknown to rule your life.

You can't make sure your husband stays sober, doesn't use pornography, handles his emotions, works on your marriage, goes to church, takes medication, gets treatment, goes to counseling, ends an affair, or makes and maintains any other positive changes. And it's not your responsibility to police him. Don't try to manage his life, check up on him, or ask him to report to you on his sobriety. It's his job to change himself and to maintain that change—whatever it takes. You aren't his counselor, teacher, mother, pastor, mentor, god, or doctor. You can share your feelings about the situation or ask reasonable questions; it's the obsession of finding out whether or not he's doing his part that you must release.

One of the conditions Connie placed on continuing her marriage with Brandon in spite of his sexual addiction was to have the Internet disconnected in her home; she did not want that temptation around. Then she found herself obsessed with whether or not he was using the Internet at work to view pornography. She came to realize that Brandon had to work out his sobriety on his own; he was the only one who could resist or succumb to the temptation. She trusted that if he did give in to it, sooner or later she would find out. In the meantime—until he had a longer track record and completed his treatment—they would not resume sexual relations.

Constant worrying and wondering will not give you the peace you're looking for. On the other hand, don't ignore reality and pretend it could never possibly happen again. Face the truth that your husband could regress, and don't be blind to warning signs. Rest in the knowledge that you'll be able to deal with it because you're not in the same place you were before. You know now that you have choices and control over your own life. Continue to maintain strong boundaries, use these principles, take care of yourself, and reach out to your support network. Rest in the fact that things out of your control are in God's hands.

Avoid Major Life Changes

Move slowly with big decisions like moving, buying a new house, quitting your job, separation or divorce proceedings, having a baby, merging bank accounts, giving him control over large amounts of your money, and so on. Don't make the mistake of thinking that a bigger house, a baby, or moving to another town will fix your marriage.

Changing outside circumstances will not fix inner problems. If things start falling apart, you'll be in an even more difficult position if you've taken on extra debt, had another child, moved to a new city, quit your job, or further complicated your situation in any way. There's plenty of time to make all these decisions when your husband has a sustained track record of healthy change under his belt.

Donna realized when Bob got out of the rehabilitation center for the third time that there were no guarantees he would stay sober, but she believed this time might be different. Bob wanted to move to Florida to work in his father's business, but Donna was not willing to move away from her family, because if Bob relapsed and they separated, she knew she would need her family's support. Bob wasn't happy with her decision, but Donna knew moving at this time was just too risky for her.

Rebuild Trust Slowly

If your husband assures you that he will change, remember—"a righteous man is cautious in friendship" (Prov. 12:26). Let your trust in him be rebuilt over time as he demonstrates a consistent track record. Trusting someone who has been untrustworthy is unwise until you have proof of change. While you wait for him to establish a record of dependability, take care of yourself. Don't do anything to risk your mental, emotional, physical, spiritual, or material safety.

Heal Past Wounds

It takes courage to face the pain of the past, but it's possible to heal from almost anything if both of you are willing to do the work. It won't be an easy process, and it won't always go smoothly.

In order to heal, you and your husband will need to discuss your past hurts. But it's not reasonable to go back and try to resolve everything in your past. Melanie wanted Jerod to admit all the times he had let her down over their ten-year marriage. Jerod felt overwhelmed and defensive. She realized that she would have to settle for the fact that he was willing to admit that he mistreated her and was willing to make changes in the way he treats her today. In Isa. 57:16 the Lord says, "I will not accuse forever, nor will I always be angry, for then the spirit of man would grow faint before me."

Even after the major problems are resolved, your husband isn't going to be everything you want him to be, and you aren't going to be everything he would like you to be. When you reach the point of accepting each other as imperfect people who will sometimes disappoint, it brings healing to you both.

There are some painful memories that time will not completely erase. Even though you would like to forget certain events, from time to time they'll come to mind. In fact, the more emotion associated with the event, the stronger the memory. When painful memories surface, you can choose how you deal with it. If you dwell on it, old feelings, resentments, and pain will be stirred up. The best thing for you to do is forgive, put it in the past, and move on. Apply the principles of Phil. 4:8 to think about what is true, noble, right, pure, lovely, admirable, excellent, and praiseworthy. Use the memory to thank God for how far He has brought you and the good that has come from the bad times.

Valerie didn't want a divorce when she asked Phil to leave the home after learning of his affair. When Phil was repentant and broke off the affair, she willingly took him back, yet she struggled with forgiveness and letting go of the pain, even though Phil was very supportive of her feelings. Valerie finally decided to refuse to let her mind imagine Phil with the other woman. Instead, she thanked God that Phil had broken off the relationship and that her marriage was being restored. In time, the memories began to fade.

Joseph was sold into slavery by his brothers and was then thrown into prison because he refused to sleep with Potiphar's wife (Gen. 37 and 39). When the opportunity for revenge presented itself, Joseph chose to view through God's eyes the wrongs that had been done to him. He recognized that God in His sovereignty allowed it and used it for His purposes and the good of others. As Joseph said, "You intended to harm me, but God intended it for good to accomplish what is now being done" (Gen. 50:20). Taking that perspective over all the negative things your husband has done to you allows you to fully heal.

Surrender Disappointment

If your husband gets worse and refuses to get help, and your marriage ends in separation or divorce, how do you handle the disappointment? You submit to God, do what's right, and continue to trust Him to redeem even this. He will still restore your life and use you for His glory. He will have compassion for you and be near you in your brokenness. He will not abandon you or leave you alone. He will continue to supply your needs and to mold you into a woman of dignity.

God does not hold the failure of your marriage over you as a life sentence of despair and brokenness. He knows the weakness of sinful people. He knows that sin-hardened hearts cause divorce. He doesn't hate the divorced person; He hates the brokenness and hurt that come from divorce. There's still a future of hope, purpose, and restoration for you.

The last thing Shelly wanted was a divorce. As a mother of two young children, she knew it was not going to be easy. Yet, she knew she had no other choice. Her husband, Todd, had left their home a year earlier and was living with his girlfriend. It was time for Shelly to start a new life. She filed for divorce, moved home to her parents, and returned to school to finish her degree. She knew God had a plan and would rebuild her life.

As Matt's verbal abuse of Ann spilled over onto their teenage daughters, Ann knew she had to leave him. Things were getting worse, and Matt refused to address the issue or get help. "I know God understands," Ann told me. "He wants me to protect my children. I tolerated it in the past, but I know putting my girls through this is no longer the right thing to do. I know God has a good future for my daughters and me."

Comfort Others

Because of your journey and the difficulties you've experienced, you can bring comfort and hope to others who are hurting. "Praise be to the God and Father of our Lord Jesus Christ, the Father of compassion and the God of all comfort, who comforts us in all our troubles, so that we can comfort those in any trouble with the comfort we ourselves have received from God (2 Cor. 1:3-4). "Encourage one another and build each other up, just as in fact you are doing" (1 Thess. 5:11).

No life experience is a waste if it can be used to help others. "God [uses] the weak things of the world to shame the strong" (1 Cor. 1:27). There are millions of other women in difficult marriages who are hurting, broken, and confused. Some of them are within your circle of contact right now. When you're willing to reach out and be used, God will give you the opportunity. When you let God use your pain to help others, you'll understand His redemptive purpose in your life and be able to rejoice.

Rejoice over Redemption

"The LORD works out everything for his own ends—even the wicked for a day of disaster" (Prov. 16:4). God redeems and restores—even when you sin and make bad choices that affect your life and the lives of others, even when your husband sins and causes you to bear the effects of his sin. God's purpose is to restore you to himself, sanctify you, and mold you into the image of His Son so that His love and salvation might be demonstrated to the world. Allow God to use both the good and bad in your life to mold you into a woman of dignity, even in the midst of your difficult circumstances. Then you'll fulfill God's purpose for your life.

"I will repay you for the years the locusts have eaten—the great locust and the young locust, the other locusts and the locust swarm—my great army that I sent among you. You will have plenty to eat, until you are full, and you will praise the name of the LORD your God, who has worked wonders for you; never again will my people be shamed" (Joel 2:25-26).

At the low point of my life my dreams had died—my dream of a Christian home, of using my talents to serve God in ministry, of raising my daughters to be young women with a heart for God, for a good marriage. But I've seen God restore those broken dreams and now rejoice in His redemption.

"'I know the plans I have for you,' declares the LORD, 'plans to prosper you and not to harm you, plans to give you hope and a future'" (Jer. 29:11). Regardless of the way your marriage goes, you have a Heavenly Father who loves you and wants to bless you. You do not have the guarantee of a perfect marriage but of a life with ample provision and grace from a God who loves you enough to send His Son to die for you.

Isa. 61:2-4 says that Jesus has been sent "to comfort all who mourn, and provide for those who grieve in Zion—to bestow on them a crown of beauty instead of ashes, the oil of gladness instead of mourning, and a garment of praise instead of a spirit of despair. They will be called oaks of righteousness, a planting of the LORD for the display of his splendor. They will rebuild the ancient ruins and restore the places long devastated; they will renew the ruined cities that have been devastated for generations."

You can trust God with the minute details of your life—the mistakes, failings, imperfect people, hurts, and sins. Then, when you reach the end of your life, you'll look back and see God's hand, and you'll know that He molded you and accomplished His purpose in you—even in your difficult marriage.